WHY ARE MEN
SO BLOODY STUPID?

To all my friends, especially Roger T – he knows why.

And to Jill, with love, and my thanks for all her help and encouragement

WHY ARE MEN SO BLOODY STUPID?

A Sideways Look at Modern Man

William Barnes

Poolside Publishing

Copyright © Hamer Books Ltd 2004
First published in 2004 by Poolside Publishing
P O Box 28871
London SW13 9XL

Cartoons by Tony Sullivan
Cover design by Tony Denton

Distributed by Gazelle Book Services Limited
Hightown, White Cross Mills, South Rd, Lancaster, England LA1
4XS

British Library Cataloguing in Publication Data
A catalogue record for this book is available from the British Library

ISBN 0-9528259-3-7

Typeset by Amolibros, Milverton, Somerset
This book production has been managed by Amolibros
Printed and bound by T J International Ltd, Padstow, Cornwall, UK

CONTENTS

INTRODUCTION

Over the centuries the world's most brilliant minds have grappled with many complex and intriguing questions. Does God exist? Is there life after death? What is the nature of time? How many imaginary numbers can be imagined in the space of ten seconds? Was Albert Einstein right in saying that gravity bends light? If the real Universe runs at right angles to the imaginary Universe, where does Infinity begin and end?

Every day in bars and pubs throughout the land, you will hear groups of men hammering away at these same profound questions until, at closing time, the ultimate 'big question' taxes their intellects – where can we get a really good curry before we go home?

What you don't hear them debating is the greatest of all puzzles ... Why are men so bloody stupid?

But, I believe that a bit of rigorous analysis will enable us to understand the problem, and also to propose some remedies.

First and foremost, it's SEX that makes them so bloody stupid. Sex is the driving force in virtually every man's life; it's the carburettor which channels the fuel for those frenetic pursuits of the opposite sex and drives the wheels of his destiny. It is a well-known and incontrovertible fact that the ordinary male, if he is not doing something really interesting like lining up a five-foot downhill left-to-right putt or something really creative like making up his expense account, has a sexual fantasy every twelve seconds.

In other words, all men like a shag, or as Aldous Huxley put it more elegantly, 'Man is an intelligence in servitude to his organs.' But let's not knock it; after all, it makes the world go round. But, if only the average male would try to peer through the immediate pink-tinged priapic haze and make an effort to anticipate the consequences of this obsession.

This was brought home to me very forcefully during a recent holiday in Majorca; in fact, I experienced a feeling not far removed from being socked behind the ear with a well-filled nappy. Promenading along the seafront late one afternoon, thinking only benign thoughts as I wondered where to stop for the first cocktail of the evening, I saw a young family.

The wife, in her early twenties, was sitting on the seawall and, oblivious to the enchanting seascape behind her, was gazing vacantly at the passing traffic. She was fat; too fat ever to have been asked to pose for a Michelin poster. I'm not saying that she wasn't a beautiful person, because she may well have been that rarity, but she was no sex symbol. She was dragging on a cigarette – so fiercely that I wondered if she was attempting to expel the smoke from a bodily orifice mercifully hidden from view. She remained totally indifferent to the efforts of her fit-looking, twenty-something husband/partner as he struggled to lever their two tiny squirming children out of their swimming costumes, get them dry and clothed, and to gather up their towels, beach balls, buckets, toys and all the other accoutrements of a jolly day by the sea.

Rudely open-mouthed in horror and astonishment, I stared at this poor sod, who was stupid enough to be doing what Mrs Lard-Arse should have been doing.

Like Archimedes in his bath, like Newton in his garden, like Heisenberg when he became absolutely certain about his Uncertainty Principle, like Einstein when he told his relatives about his theory of relativity, like stout Cortez when with eagle eyes he stared at the Pacific, like Bobby Charlton poised in front of his mirror and wondering where his hair had gone, a seminal question, which may also be a great truth, struck me – why are men so bloody stupid?

Why had this nice-looking young man, with all of his life ahead of him, a life which should be teeming with booze, ribaldry, good mates, and loads of uncomplicated sex with good-looking crumpet, landed himself with a slapper who was four stones overweight, and was leaving him to do all the hard graft with the two kids? Where had it all gone wrong, as the room service waiter asked George Best. The difference was that, when that question was posed to him, Best was swigging champagne with Miss World.

I had to calm an immediate attack of *angst* by rushing to the nearest bar and ordering a gin and tonic. As I gargled away, I couldn't get the image of that poor deluded fellow out of my mind. A man who'd dropped himself right in the mire, and probably had no idea how to get out of it. I suppose he could shoot himself, but that is a bit drastic; maybe he could flee to some far and uncharted corner of the world.

1. SEX

Maybe the woman by the Majorcan beach had been a svelte and lively bit of skirt when her man had first met her. That's an awful big maybe, and she was the living and conclusive truth that most crumpet doesn't stay that way. All men should heed this warning: virtually every long-legged filly, whose trim arse you used to fondle and snuggle and nuzzle, eventually grows and grows to the size of a Co-op horse, with a backside to match. One evening in a pub, a sage old man stopped me in my tracks. He spotted me leering at a young woman whose arse was superbly stretching the tight confines of a pair of jeans, and said, 'they strip off twice as big, son'. You can't buy that kind of wisdom.

However, the poor mutt on that Majorcan beach was no more stupid than the refined and reputable England football manager, Mr Sven Goran Ericsson. That epitome of the ice-cool, philosophical Swede was daft enough and horny enough to get into a muck-sweat over a Swedish lingerie model, whose other claim to fame was that she'd once been a weather girl; that is, until she found an easier and more lucrative profession – as a TV presenter and, wait for it, as an author.

Mind you, Sven Goran is no matinée idol, is he? In fact, he reminds me of the man who stacks the shelves at IKEA; he has all the charisma of a scoutmaster at a Mormon jamboree. Did Sven really think that the lovely Ulrika found him irresistible? Did it not occur to him that her willingness to make the two-backed beast with him might help her, one day, to flog a shag-and-tell book and to sell the serial rights for zillions to a national newspaper?

Sven, why were you so bloody stupid?

And have you noticed that the gloss has faded from Sven's much-heralded managerial skills? Nowadays, his laid-back nonchalance seems more like inertia, his refusal to get ruffled more like ineptitude and a lack of stomach for the fight. He showed minimal managerial skills during the Euro 2004 tournament; when decisive leadership was desperately needed, he was found wanting. In my view, he couldn't motivate a flea to jump on to a dog's back. If the Football Association had really wanted a turnip in charge of the England team, there are dozens of managers they could have employed at a fraction of the price.

Ericsson's dalliance with Chelsea also leaves a nasty taste in the mouth, too, doesn't it? When the Football Association learned that he might jump ship for a share of 'Chelski's' billions, instead of showing him the door, they increased his wages. What's the price of loyalty these days? Nobody in the sleazy world of football would know the answer, even if they understood the question.

* * *

The male royals haven't covered themselves with glory either, have they?

I think Prince Charles has many virtues; he has a well-judged contempt for modern architecture for a start. But, when he set out to choose a mate, he let himself be bullied by his dad, which isn't surprising because Phil the Greek is a tough customer, who also has the reputation of being a bit of a 'ladies' man', to use a suitably polite expression. So, why didn't he pass on some of that hard-won sexual wisdom to his son? Instead, he fitted him up with Diana, a princess with only one gift – for her own publicity.

And fancy marrying into a family like the Spencers. Always look at the parents and the siblings before committing yourself. You were a mug, Charlie. There was only one suitable candidate for Queen-in-Waiting and that was Joanna Lumley. Phwhoarrr. I suppose she would have been expected to change her name. Queen Joanna doesn't sound quite right– but it sounds a damn sight righter than Queen Camilla.

What about Randy Andy? One of the younger sons of Ma'am and Phil, with no responsibilities, he should have looked forward to a charmed life of willing crumpet and high living. So what does the royal wally do? He marries a floozy with all the style of a barmaid from darkest and deepest Essex.

As for Prince Edward, well, he's a bit odd, isn't he? No wonder he went into showbiz. Only a woman as fiercely ambitious as Sophie would have taken him on. One cannot help but speculate whether she has the brains to go with the ambition. She was conned by a journalist posing as a rich Arab, for God's sake, and couldn't wait to massage his ego in return for a fat fee.

Then there was Boris Becker. He was a great tennis player, but five seconds in a broom cupboard with a 'model' prompted a divorce from his wife, Barbara, who benefited to the tune of around £10 million – at about two million quid a stroke, that's a very expensive shag. No wonder they call him 'Boom Boom'. Since I am of a charitable cast of mind, I think he must be claustrophobic; having been lured into a confined space by a lubricious bit of skirt,

"I'm pleased to inform you that your X-Ray results are perfectly normal, Mr Hart."

he had to get it over and done with quickly before panic set in. To give Boris his due, he still likes to joke about his experience. The other day he remarked: 'I just have to remember that restaurants are for eating in and nothing else.'

And what about Angus Deayton? He had one of the easiest jobs in showbiz– reading the links on Have I Got News For You for forty grand a show, or some such ludicrous sum. But he blew it all away for – allegedly, to use one of his favourite words – getting too fond of recreational drugs and shagging toms.

IMPORTANT LESSON NUMBER ONE

If you are over forty years of age and have an income of more than £100,000 a year, and some lovely bit of skirt hangs on your every word, makes it clear that she finds you so amazingly clever and funny as to be well-nigh irresistible, that she sees you as a mélange of Tom Cruise, George Clooney, Michael Owen and Tom Stoppard, don't believe a word of it. DON'T BE SO BLOODY STUPID. SHE'S AFTER YOUR MONEY.

Just enjoy slipping her a crippler and then get back to your favourite bar.

* * *

Here is some free advice for you. Women's names reveal a great deal. Not just about the social aspirations of their parents, but about themselves. I have done years of selfless research on the subject and have been able to refine the whole thing down to a SHAG GRID. Below you will see a list of the more common female names and their shag quotient from nought to one hundred...

...The latter figure being the measure for a woman who charvers away like a demented stoat fresh from ingesting a large quantity of the best quality Colombian cocaine. If you meet a woman who has altered her name slightly – from Linda to Lindy, for example, or from Jenny to Jeni – you should double the shag quotient, because these women are serious contenders for 'bonkstress of the decade'. Hold on to your hat and pray that you are up to the task.

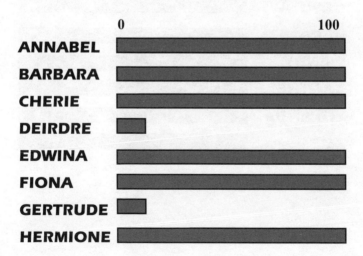

IMOGEN ▊▊▊▊▊▊▊▊▊▊▊▊▊▊

JENNY ▊▊▊▊▊▊▊▊▊▊▊▊▊▊

KATRINA ▊▊▊▊▊▊▊▊▊▊▊▊▊▊

LINDA ▊▊▊▊▊▊▊▊▊▊▊▊▊▊

MARILYN ▊▊▊▊▊▊▊▊▊▊▊▊▊▊

NINA ▊▊▊▊▊▊▊▊▊▊▊▊▊▊

OLIVIA ▊▊▊▊▊▊▊▊▊▊▊▊▊▊

Q I can't think of one, except for Queen Elizabeth and I have no intention of speculating about her private life.

RACHEL ▊▊▊▊▊▊▊▊▊▊▊▊▊▊

SARAH ▊▊▊▊▊▊▊▊▊▊▊▊▊▊

THERESA ▊▊▊▊▊▊▊▊▊▊▊▊▊▊

URSULA ▊▊▊▊▊▊▊▊▊▊▊▊▊▊

VERA ▊▊▊▊▊▊▊▊▊▊▊▊▊▊

WENDY ▊▊▊▊▊▊▊▊▊▊▊▊▊▊

XANTHE ▊▊▊▊▊▊▊▊▊▊▊▊▊▊

YOLANDE ▊▊▊▊▊▊▊▊▊▊▊▊▊▊

ZOE ▊▊▊▊▊▊▊▊▊▊▊▊▊▊

2. RANDOM THOUGHTS ABOUT LOVE AND COURTSHIP

When I was an unmarried man in my twenties, I used to meet a group of close friends every weekend. The usual pattern was to get outside a gallon or so of beer, and then to move on to a party, of which there was never a scarcity. Among those friends was a man who seemed terrifically old and wise; he was at least thirty years of age. Pete's inevitable practice, if he struck lucky with a woman and got into her bed, was to do his best and then head for home for a good night's rest.

Romantic young man that I was, I was puzzled by his casual, even perfunctory, treatment of his conquests. And it hardly seemed good value to me; after all, you've spent time and effort chatting the girl up, haven't you? What about the dawn patrol, I asked him, and one more after the late breakfast she's cooked for you and before you meet the lads in the pub? Like a battle-hardened old soldier regarding a raw and eager recruit, he looked at me pityingly, and shook his head. 'Look,' he said, 'you can always go back another time for a quick one, but if you stay the night, she'll want a cuddle and then (and his face paled) she'll want to discuss your relationship. Get out, my boy, while the going is good.' I think he added other soldierly advice about re-charging the batteries and keeping your powder dry; by the way, he'd never fired a shot in anger.

Pete might have known where the G-spot is; but I never asked him, nor anyone else. Anyway, who gives a fuck.

However, I was once daft enough to ask him about the sensitive question of foreplay. It's simple, he told me, get your trousers off as quickly as possible without making a fool of yourself by tripping over them.

* * *

Bondage is a tricky subject, isn't it? I have a mate whose girlfriend wanted to tie him up; admittedly with silk ropes, so she had a touch of class. Not bloody likely, he said, and I don't blame him. Never ever let yourself get that far into a woman's power. God knows what she might get up to.

Farting is a problem, too, isn't it? Especially in bed. Men fart, particularly after a belly-full of beer and a plateful of curry. Women don't fart (not that is, until you marry them) and they don't want you to fart. A misplaced anal blast in the hearing of a new bit of crumpet can cause problems, as one of my male relations discovered on the first night of a week's skiing holiday in Aspen, Colorado. He let one go in bed (after sex, I hope, otherwise it would have been very rude) and his lady-love left him in the morning as a result. She was an American, and they can be very prudish. It served him right that it was gay week in Aspen.

* * *

The right words can add immeasurably to the power and effectiveness of the courtship ritual. Will Shakespeare obviously had some damsel or other in his sights when he wrote: 'Shall I compare thee to a summer's day? Thou art more lovely and more temperate.' Old Will knew how to get his thumbs under the knicker elastic, didn't he? However, when an old friend of mine entered a competition in a South Wales newspaper for the best love letter, he wrote the most pithy sentence in the history of courting. It went as follows: 'I love you so much, I can't shit.' What poetry, what power, what command of the finer feelings. Oddly enough, the newspaper did not print this *cri de coeur*.

On another occasion, I heard him chatting up a girl who was a secretary – in the days when a secretary was expected to take dictation *and* a good grope from the boss without whingeing about sexual harassment. This master of the romantic phrase told her that he would 'love to be a key on your typewriter'. You can't beat such beautiful spontaneity.

3. WEDDINGS

A wedding can be fun, as long as it's someone else's. And parents often like them; they are mightily relieved to be seeing the back of a son or daughter and are praying that the marriage lasts.

Above all, the guests are looking forward to a top-class piss-up at someone else's expense. There is also the chance of a quick bonk at a wedding, since inhibitions seem to drop away. It's not just the alcohol which induces this devil-may-care, roger-me-rotten feeling; there is something rare and indefinable at work, some benign influence which makes a wedding such a good hunting ground for randy bastards of all sexes.

The wedding service is always good for a laugh, too. There is usually a fumbling geriatric in charge, who looks as though he clears a gallon of communion wine every day. Years ago, our friends, Nigel and Suzanna, got hitched and the vicar called them 'John and Joanna' right through the ceremony. Not that I noticed because, as I thumbed through the Good Book, I turned the pages to the prophet Isaiah and found the secret of golf. 'Strengthen ye the right hand,' wrote Isaiah, and shone a blindingly clear light on the whole complex subject.

When you arrive at the reception – which, after all, is the whole point of the occasion – it's always a shrewd move to slip a tenner into the hand of one of the waiters and ask him to 'look after you'. In other words, his job for the foreseeable future is to make sure that *your* glass is always topped up to the brim – and especially while you are waiting for the interminable business of the wedding photographs and the video recording of the great day to end. This can even involve the use of a white open-topped Roller, surely the ultimate vulgarity. As a guest at one wedding I attended said wearily as, with raging thirsts, we hung around, 'we're not guests, we're extras in a movie.'

However, now is the time to have a good look at the runners and riders, and try to decide who might be in the market for a sly bonk. But don't make your move too early.

Speeches are an inevitable part of a wedding and they are usually appalling, a series of embarrassingly unfunny tales about the bride and groom. If you have to do a speech, prepare well (it's polite), keep it short (everyone will adore you for that), and don't use any rude words because there are usually women and children present.

Whatever you do, don't start off, as a friend of mine once did, as follows: 'On her wedding day every bride looks gorgeous.' He paused, to milk the oohs, the aahs and the sighs. At this stage, the speaker, a good-looking lad in his twenties, was an odds-on favourite to have a jaunty tune played on his 'pink oboe' by any two or three of the randy married and divorced women who were present. Unfortunately, he followed up his very promising start with the following punch-line: 'I wonder why there are so many ugly wives in the world then.' The appalled silence was, fortunately, soon broken by ripples of laughter from some of the ruder male guests. Although I snickered with the rest, I realised that his chances of a bit of extra-marital had disappeared like a fart in a stiff breeze.

Here I must draw your attention to a very important lesson.

IMPORTANT LESSON NUMBER TWO

On the wedding day, the bridegroom should never try to get his leg over any of the bridesmaids, nor, indeed, over anyone except his bride.

That might seem so crassly obvious that it doesn't need to be said. Don't you believe it, because, a couple of decades ago, a friend of mine failed to observe that simple courtesy.

His wedding reception was being held in the basement of a large London flat and most of us were more than a little surprised when his bride did not put in an appearance. We noticed that he took a long telephone call at some stage, and we speculated whether the bride had had an accident; but we didn't like to ask, just in case it spoiled the occasion. Anyway, I reckon that both parties to a marriage should present themselves at the reception – but I am one of the great romantics.

It later transpired that the blushing bride had been tripping gaily along the pavement towards the reception (and don't ask me why she had left the side of her adoring husband – you know what women are like) and happened to glance into the basement. She saw her man in an eager embrace with the matron-of-honour, his tongue probing her mouth with sufficient gusto to unseat her tonsils.

I suppose I didn't blame her for turning tail, but she missed a bloody good party. They got divorced eventually.

4. MARRIAGE

Before you take the plunge into what can become the icy and choppy waters of marriage, I ask you to ponder this well-used adage: the cheapest fuck is the one you pay for. A friend of mine who lived in the Far East for nearly twenty years is very fond of that pearl of wisdom and, giggling the while, he usually follows it with the following injunction about the three Fs: if it flies, floats or fucks, then rent it. Over the years, I have tried to make him into a nicer person; alas, without success, although he did recently admit, with a touch of sadness, that his pragmatic approach has had an adverse effect on his conversational skills. These days his only chat-up line is 'How much?'

Nevertheless, this is a tricky subject, because there is no doubt that the average man and woman want a stable relationship; and the most stable relationship two people of the opposite sex can have is through marriage.

Except that it isn't. The divorce figures make

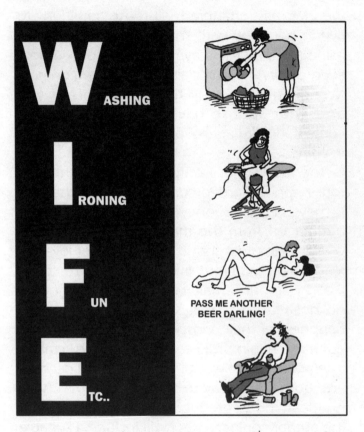

sobering reading – last year over 150,000 couples called it a day; and one in three marriages in the UK ends in divorce (the figure in the USA is one in two). All those dreams of wedded bliss shattered, all those ambitions to live in harmony with the 'wonderful kids' cast aside (and, by the way, have you noticed how every adult American claims to have two or more 'wonderful kids'?), all those thoughts of you and your spouse having a protracted and contented 'third age' of pottering about together in ruins.

The fact is that I only know about three or four happily married couples; most of the rest, if they had the money or the energy, would bugger off from the marital home tomorrow, giving forth great shouts and huzzas of joy, and lead totally different lives. But they're stuck, feeling a vague malaise that they cannot, or do not want to, analyse. It's an itch on the periphery of their consciousness and they can't quite reach it in order to give it a good scratch.

A poem which was published several decades ago goes some way to summing it up. I have no idea who wrote it or where I saw it, but, if the author contacts me, I will include a suitable acknowledgement in the next edition of this book.

After describing himself as 'an old man with a dirty mind', the writer tells us that he is 'caged in a useless job, with a graceless wife' and that he's 'tired of living but still full of life.' And here comes the really poignant bit, as he continues:

> 'And there was she with long fair hair,
> Carefree grace and a laughing air.
> I know now tigers feel no rage,
> Pacing endlessly round their cage.
> Only despair, despair, despair.'

It is not a work of genius, but made a distinct impression on me all those years ago. Isn't it sad? Such a lament for lost youth and for ambitions long discarded. And that's how most men feel after what seems to have been an eternity of marriage. So, don't be so bloody stupid, do something about it.

* * *

If your marriage is to stand a cat in hell's chance – and most of them don't – you owe it to yourself to choose your mate with extreme caution. That sounds obvious, doesn't it? But how many marriages are conceived, just like so many children, in an engulfing flush of lust mistaken for romance? The women's magazines have a lot to answer for, since they peddle the impossible dream of endless and effortless marital bliss; it's a heartless journalistic con-trick because that sort of dewy-eyed optimism isn't worth a fast fuck in the back of a Ford Mondeo.

Important Lesson Number Three

Romance works very well during a two-hour film – but a marriage has to last a lot longer.

Like most of the things that are worthwhile, you have to work for success in marriage. It's not as automatic as an early morning hard-on, which is called being 'piss-proud' where I come from. It doesn't just happen.

One of the biggest dangers to a marriage, especially if the couple is relatively young, is the assumption that they are going to do everything together. Of course, they will do lots of things together, but not everything, because that will put an intolerable strain on the relationship.

It is vital to lead separate lives to a certain extent; otherwise you will stifle each other, and grow bored with each other very quickly. You must have some interests in common; it can't just be sex, can it? Otherwise, why would you have bothered to get together in the first place? It might be good food, if she can cook; or travel, if she's rich; or going to the theatre or the opera; or something simple, like playing tennis together. But, above all, it's crucial to have different interests and to pursue them separately because they will help to refresh your relationship. Do you ever notice the couples who can sit through a whole meal in a restaurant without speaking to each other? They're the ones who did everything together and have now run out of conversation; unfortunately, they have also lost interest in each other.

* * *

One of the deadliest dangers known to man is a woman's obsessive need to get him out of the sphere of influence of his mates. To her, no matter how vivacious she has seemed in their presence in the past, they are the most insidious threat to her relationship with the man she intends to mould to her way of life. *Her* friends are to be the important people in both your future lives; *your* friends are drunks, lechers, small-time crooks, as unreliable as London buses, impractical, and, above all, dangerous.

It is very well summed up in one of Malcolm Hamer's excellent crime novels, *A Deadly Lie*. Our hero, Chris Ludlow, has realised that his latest girlfriend wants him to herself, and to herself alone; he begins to understand just how perilous the situation has become:

> 'I had seen the insidious process affect one or two friends in the past, when the new woman in his life slowly set out to alter him: an emotional remould. At first there were only trivial changes: he was not available quite so often for a game

of golf on Saturday; a quick drink after work was not so easily arranged; the weekend's golf at Le Touquet was out of the question. Within a few months you noticed that "old Mike" always seemed to be out to dinner or away for the weekend with her friends. A year or two later you were hard-pressed to remember what you had in common and certainly you had very little now; especially when the children came along and he gave up golf and rugby for their sakes.'

That sums it up very neatly.

IMPORTANT LESSON NUMBER FOUR

When you get married, lead your own life as an individual as well as one half of a couple.

Once it is known that a couple are planning to get married, the family and feminazi juggernaut rolls out of the garage and flattens all in its path, particularly the male part of the partnership. Remember well that the feminazi's burning desire is to ensure that you do not escape the process that will 'adjust' you – from carefree and priapic bachelor to careworn father and family man.

Don't succumb. There is always a way out. It may take a level of courage that would make Clint Eastwood blanch, but you can do it. Say that you've made a mistake and then head for the door. A bit of ducking and weaving, as if you've just throated a gallon of strong beer, might be in order at this stage. In fact, if you make good your escape, phone up your mates, those vile, lecherous, cerebrally-challenged idiots, and make sure that you do have a gallon of Dog's Bollocks bitter; there will never be a more appropriate time to celebrate.

Two of my friends had second thoughts about their forthcoming marriages. The first one couldn't cope with the dire consequences of a premature withdrawal (which was odd, since he was an 'occasional' Catholic and should have been used to such practices) and went ahead. At the post-marriage celebration, he confessed to one of my brothers that the marriage was 'the worst day's work' he'd ever done. You may call me a romantic old fool, but I don't think that's the ideal way to start your married life. He's divorced now, by the way.

The second one was about to marry a French girl and the wedding was planned to be a very big social event in Paris. This friend had buckets of courage, or maybe buckets of French fizz inside him, because he pulled out on the morning of the wedding. Perhaps he said, '*C'est magnifique, mais ce n'est pas le mariage pour moi.'* Perhaps not. Anyway, I've often wondered what they did with all the food and booze – no doubt, since they were Frogs, they went ahead and had a party. Funnily enough, this friend was a Catholic, too. Even more oddly, he married the girl a few months later – at a quiet ceremony. Maybe they kept the presents on one side, just in case.

IMPORTANT LESSON NUMBER FIVE

Even when the wedding juggernaut is running out of control, you can always toss yourself off.

Headache? .... Again?

5. PREGNANCY

It happens, doesn't it? A few moments of thoughtless pleasure after you've given the 16 degree Argentinian merlot too thorough a walloping and, a few weeks later, the wife/crumpet tells you she's got one in the oven. She's pleased and, since you are a gentleman, you join in her pleasure. Don't make the mistake one of my friends made when his wife announced that she was pregnant; he told her bluntly to get rid of it. That was not the reaction of a gentleman, but in his defence he had just returned from an arduous business trip to the Far East and I can only excuse his forthrightness (and honesty is a virtue, even if tact should always moderate it) by the strain imposed on him by his sterling work in foreign parts.

In fact, there is a silver lining within this potentially shitty situation. For some reason this is a time when women become very keen on shagging. For a few weeks, you can roger the crumpet up hill and down dale to your heart's content. No orifice need remain unplumbed.

Some psychologists have recently claimed to have detected 'memory loss and lack of concentration' in pregnant women; they call it 'nappy brain' or 'preg head' syndrome. Don't be stupid enough to buy that one, because your crumpet will run you ragged if you do. Women don't get more stupid when they get one in the oven; on the contrary, they get more cunning and manipulative, and you, dear sirs, will be the primary target of their Macchiavellian machinations. Just ignore their attempts to gain your sympathy; get on with your life as normally as you can.

You now enter a period of your life when you are in maximum danger from the feminazis. They see a chance to reclaim one of their own – your crumpet – and to smother her in all the mush that inevitably accompanies pregnancy. This is when, in their opinion, you can resume your rightful place in the scheme of things – in a back seat while your woman fulfils her glorious destiny, which is to become a Mum. But they will have their designs on you, too. Although you are regarded as totally subsidiary to this noble aim – you grunted and groaned a few million sperm into a (presumably) willing womb – they will aim to envelop you in the same soft and downy cloud of gloop, to destroy you as an entity, to make you subservient to the whole long and boring process of pregnancy.

Important Lesson Number Six

Don't give an inch. Now is the time to reinforce your status as a man. Get your intake of alcohol up and your golf handicap down.

This is when I ask you to think about one of the great men in history, Genghis Khan. I read the other day that one in twenty men is, by some quirk of the genetic chain, descended from him. So, he must have done an enormous amount of shagging. But, when he wasn't engaged in a bit of charvering, the Universal Ruler, as he was called, created one of the greatest empires in history, an empire that extended from the Black Sea to the Pacific. He managed it without the help of cruise missiles, tanks, or helicopter gunships. Not only that, but he organized his territories into states which lasted a lot longer than most Asiatic empires.

AND GENGHIS WOULD BE APOPLEPTIC WITH RAGE AT HOW HIS PROGENY HAS TURNED OUT.

He would be particularly enraged at how modern man has thrown in the towel in the battle of the sexes.

I blame the 1960s. That was when a new

"It's late afternoon! Shouldn't the hunter, gatherer,
be HUNTING, GATHERING by now?"

and glorious freedom seemed to brighten the skies; the hems on the mini-skirts went skywards, and so did the self-confidence of a new generation – 'bliss was it in that dawn to be alive, but to be young was very heaven', as Wordsworth put it a couple of hundred years ago.

Unfortunately, all that women's lib crap arrived at the same time, and that's when the natural order of things went pear-shaped. Some of the women were daft enough to believe in it; the trouble was, so did some of the men. They allowed the monstrous regiment of women, marshalled originally by that bossy bit of skirt from the colonies, Germaine Greer, and all the ranks of the feminazis who have followed in her wake, to take away man's traditional status.

The great Genghis Khan knew all about man's status. Man is a hunter/gatherer, who, when he is not hunting and gathering, likes nothing better than to loll around the fire, a glass of something good in one hand, his other hand scratching his bollocks or his arse, and telling ridiculously boastful tales of his prowess as hunter, gatherer and shagger. Christ, a bloke's got to relax, hasn't he? Women are there to do the cooking, pleasure their men and look after the kids.

If dear old Genghis were around today, he would take a look at gutless modern man and, despite having a well-documented soft side to his character, would undoubtedly nominate every fifth one to be taken away and torn to shreds by his packs of Mongolian killer-mastiffs. He would probably be so upset that he'd rush off and conquer China all over again.

The Great Man would undoubtedly have been as horrified as I was when I read that a recent study (it was done by some American academics, so I'm treating their report with a lorry-load of salt) has concluded that British men are among 'the top home-helps of Europe'. Apparently, some of these spineless wimps even take their turn in changing their babies' nappies; and only the Danish male is more egalitarian in the home. That makes you think, doesn't it? That Britain is on a par with a nation like Denmark. Can you think of anyone of distinction from Denmark? Of course you can't – except for that bloke, Hamlet. And it needed a ghost-writer, Will Shakespeare no less, to make him famous. Come back, Genghis Khan, we need you now – desperately.

* * *

In his interesting book, *Y: The Descent of Man*, Steve Jones writes about modern man's declining sperm count. During a period from the 1950s to the mid-1970s, the numbers generated both by American and British males had declined by a half and a wider study confirmed the same startling figures over a longer period. By the end of this century, argues Jones, Western Man's sperm will be inert; with one bound, the population crisis will be solved.

And no wonder the poor old male will be firing blanks – it's because he's been emasculated by the voracious ranks of the feminists whose sole aim is to rule the world. However, read on, because there are many ways in which men can fight back, so let's continue with the important subject of pregnancy. You will now be under intense pressure to become involved in many of its tedious rituals, and eventually in the turmoil of childbirth.

IMPORTANT LESSON NUMBER SEVEN

Pregnancy is WOMAN'S WORK. Keep well clear.

The place for you throughout this traumatic time is down at the pub and the club. Keep out of the way, and make sure you get plenty of bets on the sex of the child as soon as this has been established by the amniocentesis procedure.

At some stage, a health visitor will hove into view and discuss the importance of your accompanying your wife to ante-natal classes and taking a full part in the pregnancy process. She will give you a little booklet about it. Please refer to IMPORTANT LESSON NUMBER SEVEN (above). In other words, tell her that this is woman's work and toss the booklet into the nearest waste-paper basket. If you can do this with all the nonchalance of James Bond tossing his trilby on to the hat-stand in Miss Moneypenny's office, so much the better. You should then make a smooth exit to the nearest bar, or consult your cellar book and speculate aloud about which vintage champagne you will broach with your mates when your *son* is born (at this point a spirited rendition of the first few lines of 'My Boy Bill' is perfectly in order). Or turn on the TV and watch some sport.

* * *

By the way, let me warn you very sternly not to go near a new magazine called *Dad*. The very title reveals just how deeply patronising the concept is – and you won't be surprised to hear that the great British public is paying for this pap.

The Nanny State is in action yet again, via a magazine which has the bloody cheek to purport to tell men how to be proper, caring fathers. It's a colossal waste of time and money; everyone knows that men do not want to read about parenthood. They want to read about sport and scandal, and look at photographs of girls with big knockers.

No doubt, Prime Minister Blair gave his approval to the idea of *Dad*, because he has been at great pains to demonstrate that caring side of his own character, while still trying to be the Big Swinging Dick of international politics, along with his mate, George Bush. Actually, Tony, I think we'd all prefer you to concentrate on important matters like running our country. Er, on second thoughts …

Mind you, you've got to feel sorry for Blair, haven't you? He looks knackered all the time, and he has to masquerade as Super-Dad, too. No wonder he and Cherie acquired a 'lifestyle guru'. She was a topless model once, I heard, so old Tony's not so daft, after all. Maybe that's why he's got heart palpitations; know what I mean, Tony?

And he gets out and about a lot, doesn't he? I suspect he wants to get away from his missus. Recently, I read what she listed as her recreations in Who's Who. Wait for it – theatre, the arts, keeping fit, enjoying my children. Blimey, how boring can you get? She sounds like one of those aspiring beauty queens, who used to be interviewed on the telly by Michael Aspel. The only item missing is 'I love to travel'; but she does plenty of that. At whose expense, I wonder.

However, let's get back to *Dad*. They have roped in several fascinating and important people to encourage us lesser mortals to be better at dad-dom. First, there is the footballer, David Beckham, who tells us that he is a 'hands on' father, who used to get his Versace clothing dirty when he fed Brooklyn. Then there's Colin Firth, an actor, who goes all gooey when he talks about his son.

Do the chancers who came up with the idea of *Dad* really think that people like Beckham, who was recently daft enough to spend a million quid on a ring for his wife, and like Colin Firth, an archetypal 'luvvie' who has never said anything interesting unless it has been written for him by someone else, can have any advice worthy of note for some poor bastard on a measly minimum wage who is wondering how he and his partner will cope when the baby arrives?

Treat the patronising pages of *Dad* with the contempt they deserve.

6. CHILDBIRTH

Men have been completely sucker-punched by the massed and jack-booted ranks of the feminazis over this; if this were a boxing match, it would have been stopped long ago. Every father-to-be is told that he must be present to support his wife, and to experience the miracle of birth.

Don't be so bloody stupid, this is absolute drivel. YOU DON'T HAVE TO BE THERE.

The problem is that so many men, having swallowed all this balderdash, have added to the cant that surrounds and obscures the whole subject. As I've pointed out elsewhere, if men had to give birth the human race would have died out not long after Adam and Eve had their first shag.

The whole business is much too painful and messy for a man – and he does not need to know anything about it. That's why there have always been mid*wives*, not mid*husbands*. Men are too sensitive for all that muck, blood and discomfort. And there is no reason to experience it by proxy.

Let me repeat that I am one of the great romantics; therefore, I never wanted to watch my wife, or any other woman for that matter, give birth, just as I do not want to watch her perform any of her other intimate bodily functions. OK, so some of you do, and it takes all sorts, as the philosophers say. You will find the appropriate advice in the writings of Richard Krafft-Ebing.

So, don't be so bloody stupid; do not allow yourself to be brainwashed. Get down to the pub with your mates and wait for her sister/mother/auntie to phone you. The hospital staff will thank you for staying away because the proud father-to-be is always a complete bloody nuisance in such a situation, liable to panic, to ask inconsequential and stupid questions, and to faint.

Even Jack Nicklaus, arguably the greatest of all golfers and a supreme sportsman, found the process too much for him. He attended the hospital when all five of his children were born, although in those days fathers were not allowed into the delivery room. As soon as he saw each new-born baby for the first time, the great man managed to faint. Since 'Big Jack' usually weighed in at around fifteen or sixteen stones, it must have been bloody dangerous when he measured his length on the hospital floor. He tells this endearing story against himself, and adds that, in the end, smelling salts were always at the ready.

The point I am making is that Jack Nicklaus, a single-minded man of epic determination, was at the hospital because he wanted to be – unlike today's spineless wimps, who have been pussy-whipped into accepting that they *must* be there. The feminazi dictat rules, OK?

* * *

Tom Watson is another golfing hero of mine, a man who won the Open Championship on five occasions. But my admiration of him took a severe dent when I learned why he withdrew from the 1979 US Ryder Cup team – it was because his wife was about to give birth. Oh dear, millions of golf fans suddenly thought you'd lost the plot, Tom. What were you doing nervously pacing around a hospital waiting room when you could have been representing your country in one of the greatest of all sporting contests?

In contrast, there is an Irish golfer who had the right attitude. When his wife was about to give birth he wisely chose to play in a tournament far from home. An interviewer, a politically correct idiot, asked him whether he felt he should be at the birth. 'Yer man' replied, 'I'm out here doing my job, and she's at home doing hers.' And so say all of us men – the

ones, that is, who haven't yet thrown in the towel.

* * *

Now the tennis player, Tim Henman, has got in on the act. His lovely wife, Lucy, gave birth in 2002 and he was reported to have said: 'Nothing can compare with the arrival of your first child. Not even winning Wimbledon.' Dream on, Timmy, your chances of winning Wimbledon are about the same as mine. Stick to tennis, Tim, and don't spout claptrap about fatherhood. Anyone can be a dad, very few have your talent as a tennis player.

And our Timmy is a fine tennis player; in the last decade he has reached the quarter-finals at Wimbledon eight times, and he has gone on to reach the semi-finals on four occasions. That's a superb record, and he seems a modest sort of cove, a bit thick in that vaguely British minor public school sort of way. He's a very British sort of hero, he isn't a street-fighter like Jimmy Connors or John McEnroe; he appears rather too nice to reach the pinnacle of his sport. But I read recently that he doesn't read, that he thinks 'books are boring'. What a prattish thing to say; and it gives us an insight into why he won't reach the peaks of his sport. To adapt the celebrated dictum of the West Indian writer, C L R James, 'what does he know of tennis, who only tennis knows?'

Talking of writers, I know one. He's a great chap and his partner had a baby recently. He attended the birth, of course. The full story is that he was on his way by train to an important appointment (and writers don't get asked to important appointments very often) when his mobile phone rang. He was told that his partner was being taken to hospital, since the birth was imminent. So, he got off the train at the next stop and rushed to the hospital to be present. Snap out of it, old chap, you've been brainwashed.

* * *

Finally, we come to England's two recent cricket captains. During the highly unsuccessful tour of Australia over the winter of 2002/3, Nasser Hussain deserted the team, already at its lowest ebb after a series of defeats, because his wife was about to give birth in Perth. You were a wimp, Nasser, your place was with your demoralised team, not with your missus.

However, his wimpishness pales in comparison with that of his successor, Michael Vaughan, who actually left the field during the second Test match against New Zealand at Headingley, because his wife was about to give birth. He had a job to do as England's captain, but he put his own personal concerns first. Can you imagine Douglas Jardine leaving his team in the lurch in the middle of a Test series? Or

Freddie Trueman not turning up to open the bowling because his wife was in labour? No, of course you can't. It's as unlikely as the Duke of Wellington postponing the Battle of Waterloo because his wife was about to give birth. With Jessies like Hussain and Vaughan at the helm of English Test cricket, it's no wonder that those hard-edged Aussie buggers in the baggy green caps invariably make us look second-rate.

* * *

However, you must get involved in one supremely important battle – over the name your son and heir, or daughter, receives. I am a father and when my wife first announced that she was pregnant we fell to discussing NAMES. Normally reasonably sensible, for a woman that is, my beloved proposed Toby as a suitable moniker if the child came down the chute with some wedding tackle. 'Toby', I shrieked with vivid anguish. 'Toby', I let rip again, just in case she had not registered the extent of my dismay. 'Yes, Toby,' she said, in that infuriatingly smug and cock-sure (whoops, that adjective isn't quite right, is it?) way women assume when such matters are being discussed.

I went on at some length about the name Toby. So redolent of the chattering classes and of over-bred little twerps from the posher parts of the Home Counties. Have you ever heard of a Toby who played scrum-half for England,

IT IS SAID, AFTER THE BIRTH OF HIS NEWBORN SON, AN INDIAN WARRIOR WOULD NAME HIM AFTER THE FIRST THING HE SAW.. 'SITTING BULL'.... 'RED CLOUD'.... 'STANDING BEAR'.......

(It could be worse - imagine being called 'TOBY!')

I asked; clever cow, she pointed out that somebody called *Rupert* Moon had played in that position – and for Wales of all countries. Well, what about the great generals, statesmen, explorers, I sobbed. Toby Scott of the Antarctic, I snarled between the tears of frustration, how ridiculous can you get; Field Marshall Toby Montgomery; Sir Toby Churchill; Toby Ballesteros, Stormin' Toby Schwartzkopf. What about Sir Toby Belch, she asked.

I decided to act like a politician and just continue making my point, whatever the other person tries to say. He'll be called Archie, I continued, or Bill, or Jack. If I had known the words of that song from Rodgers and Hammerstein's wonderful musical, *Carousel*, I would have belted them out, even though singing is not one of my strong suits:

> 'I wonder what he'll think of me!
> I guess he'll call me "the old man!"
> I guess he'll think I can lick
> Every other feller's father.
> Well, I can!'

The last line would not have rung true either. But I made the strength of my feelings known to her.

The worst aspect of this harrowing discussion was that she was winding me up, because she knew the result of the amniocentesis, and that our child was a girl. I couldn't, and still cannot, comprehend how a woman could stoop to such lowly behaviour, and I'll bet you can't, either. Anyway, I still call our daughter Archie and she doesn't seem to mind.

I am making an important point here. Don't let the mother fart about with fancy names. Give the child a chance in life; he or she doesn't want to spend his or her formative years being teased to distraction, because a daft parent has named her Fifi Trixiebell or Emerald Brightstar; or named him Meadowlark Lemon or Brooklyn. And self-consciously Celtic names are a big mistake, too. I know a very nice Englishman – his name is Smith, or Atkins, or Brown, something very English anyway. When his charming Welsh wife gave birth, he allowed her to name the poor little sod something like Gwyllym ap Ceri Huw Smith. He'll have a great time at school, won't he? Nearly as good a time as the offspring of the pretentious prat of an artist who named his daughter something like Moonshine Poppy Tangerine Velvet. They're not all locked up, you know.

7. CHILDREN

Some blokes get married in order to have children and so do some women; let's hope such people meet and mate and live happily ever after. But the sad fact is, that for every marriage that survives or is even enhanced by the procreation of children, another ten are torn apart by the stresses and strains of bringing up and paying for kids. Kingsley Amis summed it up in *One Fat Englishman* as follows: 'It is no wonder people are so horrible when they start life as children.' A cynical remark, but also a wise one.

In their early days, babies may be adorable as they gurgle and grin and gesticulate and look at you as if you are the single most important person in the world – be warned, this is one of nature's tricks to make sure you stick around until they reach adulthood.

The other side of the coin is that children are remarkably like drunks. Their behaviour is erratic, to put it mildly; they always smell, they

GROUND FLOOR FLAT

FREEHOLD   **£550,000**

SPACIOUS 2 BEDROOM FLAT,
CLOSE TO TUBE. LARGE
NEWLY REFURBISHED KITHCEN,
USE OF GARDEN

HOUSE

FREEHOLD   **£892,000**

- LARGE COUNTRY RESIDENCE
- 5 BEDROOMS
- 5 RECEPTION ROOMS
- GARAGE

TOWNHOUSE

FREEHOLD   **£786,000**

- 2 RECEPTION ROOMS
- LARGE KITCHEN
- 2 DOUBLE BEDROOMS
- SOUTH FACING PATIO

SPROG

LEASEHOLD - FOR LIFE
£500,000 - £1,000,000

- NEEDS LOTS OF ATTENTION
- HIGH MAINTENENCE
- INTEREST RATES VARY ON AGE
  (USUALLY 75% APR)

fart and puke, they fall over and break things, they scatter food about the place, and they make sudden strange noises. In other words they require almost constant attention, and this is WOMAN'S WORK. Let her get on with it, and both mother and child will thank you, in the end, for staying unselfishly out of the way until the job is done.

IMPORTANT LESSON NUMBER EIGHT

Keep out of the way for the first few years – WOMAN AT WORK.

So, don't fall for it. I have lost count of the number of blokes I've known who have suddenly disappeared from view for years, sometimes for decades. Then, one day, you see one of them at a reunion or on the golf course; you ask where they've been and they say, with a sad and self-pitying half-smile, 'oh, you know, the children have been growing up, you know how it is.' They are complete Jessies.

IMPORTANT LESSON NUMBER NINE

Keep a sense of proportion. Lead a full life.

You could get lucky and spawn a pop idol, or a star footballer, tennis player or golfer, or a best-selling novelist. That is, however, highly unlikely. What you can put your ever-inflating mortgage on is that any kid worth his or her salt will cost you the thick end of half a million quid in school fees and top-of-the-range trainers before you get rid of him. *If you can get rid of him.* Cheap accommodation – cramped bed-sitters with terminally weary furniture, scrofulous flats over-crammed with ill-washed flatmates – no longer exists. So, be prepared for the fruits of your loins to hang around until well into their thirties. They will be a constant source of irritation, expense and worry.

8. HOUSEWORK

One of the great heroes of our time is a friend of mine who used to live in Los Angeles. Occasionally, we stayed with him and his wife in their agreeable home in one of the canyons near Riviera Golf Club, which is where Larry, wise man that he was, used to spend most of his waking hours.

As the light faded, Larry would return and his first action was to stroll to the mammoth refrigerator, fill a glass to the brim with ice, pour a full measure of vodka on top of the ice, settle into an armchair and wait for his evening meal to be served. I began to get an inkling of the uncompromising attitude that a man should have to housework. But he brought it home to me most pointedly a few days later.

One morning, he was up bright and early at around 10 o'clock and my wife was looking helplessly at the high-tech coffee machine. She was daft enough to ask Larry how it worked. He gave her a look that was at once uncomprehending, pitying and withering. He spoke not a word but strode to the kitchen door and gave a fortissimo shout for his own wife. Vivian rushed into the kitchen and dealt with what was WOMAN'S WORK.

What a fine and uncomplicated man; his actions encapsulate all that a male person needs to know about housework. Nothing. Don't even think about participating in such an unsuitable and unsettling pastime. Show me a man with a feather duster in his hand and I will show you an imbecile. He looks stupid and incompetent, whereas a woman with a feather duster in her hand is like Vermeer with a palette and a paint-brush, like Ernie Els with a sand-wedge at the ready, like Thierry Henry with a football at his feet, like the Pétomane with a can of baked beans in front of him. She is all smoothness and brisk efficiency, she's an artist, she's poetry in motion. Whatever you do, don't spoil it for her. That would not be kind.

As for hoovering, that is an even greater sin for a man. All that pushing and pulling can aggravate a bad back. You haven't got a bad back? Of course you have and any of that hoovering will have a severely adverse effect on your next round of golf or your next game of squash.

Never go near an iron. They are very dangerous because they get very hot, especially those steam-iron things, which whoosh and hiss in a rather menacing way. If there is a crisis and you simply must iron the front of your evening dress shirt before you go out to the golf club dinner, this is what you should do to ensure that you are never allowed near the bloody thing again. While the iron is still hot, put it down on the carpet, or better still on a pair of *her* satin kecks (I am assuming that *you* don't wear satin next to the skin). That will do the trick.

IMPORTANT LESSON NUMBER TEN

Acquire a bad back. You can easily learn all the patter about your sciatic nerves and your dodgy sacro-iliac disc. Groan a bit when you have to get up out of your armchair and rub your lower back ruminatively. A very useful tactic is to learn some stretching exercises – they're good for your golf anyway. And do them anywhere in the house where you can get in your wife's way – on the bedroom floor when she's trying to get ready to do the shopping or on the living-room floor before the in-laws arrive for lunch.

9. COOKERY

This falls into the same category as housework. Because of the glut of cookery programmes on television, we are all being brainwashed into thinking of this minor skill as a great art. It's not. It is simply about knocking up something to eat. So, if you are tempted to swagger about the kitchen and start fancying yourself as another Galloping Gourmet or Philip Harben, think again. Do you ever hear of them anymore? Of course not because, after being exposed on telly for so long, they became laughing stocks and were unable to show their faces in public. No red-blooded male, or female for that matter, would go near them.

So, don't enter the kitchen except to deal with the practicalities of keeping the booze supplies in good order, i.e. make sure there is a good supply of ice cubes, that there are plenty of cold beers in the refrigerator, and that the wines are at their correct temperatures.

Never, ever, profess any interest in how the

food you eat actually becomes the food you eat. If you do, a lifetime of culinary purgatory awaits you: the planning of menus (especially if you have Guests, in other words her mates and/or family); extended shopping trips to procure all those ingredients the existence of which you were unaware; the protracted nervous tension of actually cooking the bloody meal (especially if you have Guests); and their pitying looks as your sickeningly proud wife or partner tells them that you've done the cooking. Once she's got you wearing one of those stripey aprons, you might as well capitulate and wear some frilly knickers to go with it.

'Isn't he wonderful?' she chirrups and your Guests don't even try to hide their snickering contempt for another fuckwit who's been conned rotten by his crumpet. Cunning and slippery, she's well on her way to grooming you into her little 'house-husband'. As always, Shakespeare had a phrase for such total tossers: he called them 'cot-queans'. Nice one, Will. So, don't be bloody stupid, don't fall for it.

Don't leave all the other minor irritations out of the equation, either. Kitchens are hot and make you sweat, pans and grills are hot and will burn you at the most inopportune moments, you will cut yourself with one of those bloody sharp 'kitchen devil' knives, and those sodding onions will make you weep more tears than

when England went out of the World Cup on penalties.

Then there are chilli peppers. They are dynamite in edible form. If you are daft enough to try to de-seed and chop one, be bloody careful what you do next; don't pick your nose or touch any of your other intimate or sensitive parts (or anyone else's, for that matter) because they will burn like hell.

Then there's the washing up. If you're in the kitchen doing some cooking, you will have to clear up occasionally: 'clear as you go', as the immortal Mrs Beaton wrote. I'll bet she had an army of servants to do it for her, the complacent cow.

Then there is a major and stomach-turning danger. You might be suckered into watching a cookery programme on television, and it might be one with that squinty-eyed twerp, Jamie Oliver, who seems to be getting rather portly (and who cannot even be bothered to wear a tie or comb his hair, when he has the huge privilege of meeting the Queen – *o tempora, o mores*!); or with that tedious little *hausfrau*, Delia Smith. Mind you, someone told me she's got a gleam in her eye, when you get to know her.

Anyway, if you're sharing a house with a woman, make it very clear that you consider the kitchen to be a woman's domain. To enter it unnecessarily would be, for you, the equivalent of bursting into the bathroom and catching her shaving her bikini line or plucking the hairs from around her nipples. But, beware that, even for the most devoted disciple of Macchiavelli, this tactic will only work for a limited time.

Important Lesson Number Eleven

A man's job is to look after the beer and the wine. Never show any interest whatsoever in what your beloved is doing in the kitchen – beyond asking when your scoff will be on the table.

In the end you will be rumbled. But, you are, after all, a gent and you care for her, and you want to help. Fortunately, there are scores of ways of putting her off any thoughts of enlisting any real help from you in *her domain*.

Important Lesson Number Twelve

You can fuck up anything if you want to.

Tea and coffee. You can't mess up tea and coffee, I hear you cry timorously. Yes, you bloody well can. Don't boil the water for a start; and then leave the teabag for a while so that the water goes all scummy. If that doesn't work, always have a supply of slightly 'off' milk available and use it.

Eggs. If you are frying eggs, always break the yolk. Then drop the egg in very hot fat (keep some rancid fat handy, if you can); this ensures that the underside will be leathery and the top watery. The whole creation should look like a huge gobbet of desiccated phlegm. If you are boiling an egg, the same general principle applies: make it very hard or very watery, whichever is least appropriate. I doubt you will be asked to scramble or poach eggs – but they are even easier to fuck up.

Bacon. Serve it like hand-tooled Moroccan leather.

Toast. Make it as black as charcoal.

Fish and chicken. Cook it to the consistency of a gaucho's saddle, or leave it as raw as newly-cut tripe.

Everything else. Make it lumpy, runny, or as hard as a whore's eyes – and as unprepossessing.

10. IN-LAWS AND PROSPECTIVE IN-LAWS

This situation is always filled with real and potential dangers. If they are your 'prospectives', you don't want them to love you and you don't want them to loathe you either. It is tricky, whereas if they are your actual in-laws (even if it is only on a temporary basis), it isn't tricky at all; you don't give a bugger what they think.

I have to tell you that my own legendary patience and good humour deserted me one Christmas long ago, when my present from my in-laws was a pair of gardening gloves, whereas all the other sons-in-law received bottles of vintage port.

Never give the buggers an ounce of encouragement. Otherwise, they will be in and out of your house, making themselves at home, sympathising with their daughter and all her problems, and keeping her away from her proper duties, which are to make your life comfortable.

You have, I hope, already learned the cookery lessons outlined above. If the in-laws come visiting, you merely have to apply them more vigorously.

Despite the crass ineptitude which you have consistently demonstrated in the kitchen – you literally 'cannot boil an egg' – make a very strong and concerted bid to cook lunch or dinner for the family. The crumpet will not be keen, but tell her how hard she's been working (and so she should) and how you want to make a contribution, show her family that you really are one of the 'new men', and that you've been poring over a Delia Smith cookbook in secret anticipation of being let loose in *her domain*. Sell the idea hard, it will pay off like the winning ticket in the lottery.

Tell her that you want to do a traditional lunch: roast ribs of beef with Yorkshire pudding and all the usual trimmings. Make a big palaver about watching your sainted mother make the Yorkie pud and that, in your bachelor days, you never had a failure with it. Tell her that your toad-in-the-hole was famous amongst your mates. She'll sneer a bit because she loathes most of your mates, but that doesn't matter; keep the main objective firmly in your mind.

On the morning in question, ask her not to bother about a thing and tell her that you'd

"Bob would love you to come and stay the
weekend, mother!"

like to be left alone to create the lunch. This is what you do.

Get the vegetables on the hob three hours in advance: carrots, Brussels sprouts, and peas.

Get the beef into the oven at least four or five hours before the kick-off. If one reckons that 15 minutes per pound is about right for pink-ish beef, make sure you cook it for an hour per pound. The aim is to bear proudly to the table a wizened lump of beef which is burnt black on the outside and is as grey as a guest-house sheet on the inside. Apply the usual principles to the Yorkshire pud – burn it to a cinder or make it look like sodden lumps of white bread stained with solidified snot.

The gravy must be battleship-grey, too, with knuckle-sized lumps floating on a surface as greasy as a Teddy Boy's quiff.

The booze will not be a problem. It won't be difficult to find a watery bottle of Bordeaux, made in a dodgy year, at your local off-licence; half these wines are undrinkable and the rest are 'corked'. Tell them the wine is from an impeccable chateau, but it's 'a bit tough at the moment, you've got to let it breathe and open out'. They'll grit their teeth and drink it, however horrible it tastes.

If you do have time during your culinary labours, having told the crumpet not to touch anything in the kitchen on pain of a fine of five blow-jobs, take pa-in-law down to the local pub just before lunch and feed him three or four pints of Dog's Bollocks Bitter (6.6% strength) – or however many it takes to get him pissed. This is a bit of insurance so that the lunch is guaranteed to be an even greater shambles.

IMPORTANT LESSON NUMBER THIRTEEN

This lunch for the in-laws will accomplish two crucial things. First, you will never again be allowed even to help in the preparation of a meal. Secondly, you won't see your in-laws for a very long time.

11. DO-IT-YOUSELF

Don't, because you will do it badly and probably hurt yourself in the process. Screwdrivers in the hands of the inexpert can be deadly, and so can paintbrushes. I mean that. I tried to paint a particularly rough roughcast wall and got painter's elbow; it is much worse than tennis elbow and buggered up my golf game for several days.

I won't even state the obvious about ladders. They are lethal, especially after a long lunch. Don't be bloody stupid, get a man in to do it.

The only fun I can discern is if you can persuade your crumpet to get up a ladder. Give her a good goosing as she reaches step number five and then make good your escape to the pub. Which reminds me of the limerick about Titian, when he was mixing rose madder, and his model was poised on a ladder.

'Her position to Titian, suggested coition,
So he went up the ladder, and 'ad 'er.'

Those painters had some fun, didn't they?
And, of course, there's nothing like some really
good poetry, is there?

D.I.Y.

12. GARDENING

Don't be so bloody stupid – see my remarks above about DIY. Avoid gardening like the plague. Get a man in to do the work. You've got a bad back, haven't you? The only good thing about gardens is that, if one of those warm summer days crops up, you can relax and imbibe a few cold beers or some refreshing draughts of sauvignon, while the crumpet gets the barbecue going. When a satisfactory glow has been achieved, both to the fire and to your cheeks, you can supervise the ritual burning of the sausages and lamb chops.

Anyway, danger lurks if you take the remotest interest in the garden, and as always it emanates from the bloody TV; you might be lured into watching one of those phenomenally boring telly programmes on the subject with Alan Tithead, or whatever his name is, and that ghastly creature with the saggy knockers.

13. HEALTH AND ILL HEALTH

Some women are always ill. If it's not their period, it's their PMT, and if it's not PMT, then it's post-menstrual misery. When their fertile years have ended women take up health, or rather ill health, as a hobby. Whenever I venture out of the gates of my home and espy a group of elderly ladies, I know what they're talking about – illness. Yes, it's their favourite topic. Who's dead, who's dying, there's a lovely day, oh the cost of soapflakes, as the immortal Dylan Thomas put it, or something like it. But don't dismiss these old crones as a bunch of miseryguts with nothing in their lives except visits to their GP and bingo. You can learn from them.

IMPORTANT LESSON NUMBER FOURTEEN

If you must have a semi-permanent relationship with a woman, pick a fit one.

You don't want one who is forever trotting off to see the doctor, who faints on the Tube station, or who goes down with some inexplicable malaise at the start of a holiday. Once that pattern is established, you'll be dancing attendance on her as long as this 'steady' relationship lasts; and she'll cost you a small fortune in medical insurance. A mate of mine had a wife who was always ailing. On holiday once, she claimed that 'her bones ached' and took to her bed. Why was he stupid enough to put with her nonsense? Remember– women are as tough as a crocodile's foreskin; otherwise they wouldn't go through the agony of childbirth. It's a truism that if men had to give birth, the human race would have died out aeons ago.

Important Lesson Number Fifteen

Make illness your friend. Don't be a hero.

I have already given you some important instructions on this topic; you should by now be in full possession of 'a dodgy back', which is relieving you of any fears of having to pitch in and do anything which is physically demanding such as housework, gardening, or DIY, when all you want to do is reduce your golf handicap or increase the size of your liver by getting on the outside of a good bottle of

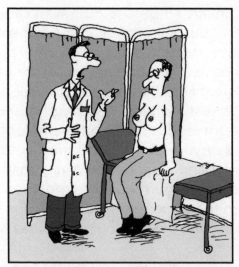

"The bad news is, you've developed breasts, Mr Peters!"

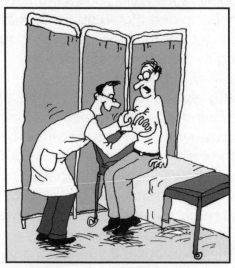

"The good news is...they're magnificent!"

Viper's Breath 16 degree Australian cab-sav.

When you have the slightest ailment, take a leaf out of the old crones' book – but only up to a point. Be subtle, and apply the precepts of the great Macchiavelli. Don't dwell on your problem, just mention it in passing and then change the subject. Go off your food a bit (make sure you have a good meal before you get home) and retire to bed earlier than usual. Tell your wife/partner/girlfriend that you're going to the spare room 'because I don't want to disturb you'. See, you're a caring man at heart.

In the morning, you will be ready to strike. When she brings your tea and newspaper, ask for a couple of pain-killers and say that you think a few hours in bed should do the trick and then you can get off to work. In fact, you won't be going to work for at least two days. If she's around, stay in bed, and get her running.

If she goes out to work, as she should, you can slip away for a game of golf or a long lunch. But don't stay out too late, because she might get home early in order to soothe your fevered brow; and beware, she might have phoned to see how you were, so cover yourself by saying that you heard the phone ringing but you were too weak to get up and answer it.

A really good puke, if you can manage it, is a potent weapon in emphasising how ill you are. While I agree that men usually only do a technicolour yawn as a result of too much booze, and therefore receive little sympathy from any quarter, let alone from the crumpet, it does help your cause when you are simulating illness. And when you call for God on the great white phone, make it loud, really loud, don't hold back – make sure you chunder for England.

On the other hand, if your spouse is ill and selfish enough to take to her bed, tell her you've got a lot on at work but you'll ask her mother to come over and look after her – or, even better, say you'll get your own mother to come over. She'll be up and about within minutes.

14. FASHION

Don't be so bloody stupid. Virtually every man on this planet is colour-blind and style-blind. You only have to look, if you can bear the shock, at the average show business occasion, an awards ceremony, for example; and the show business fraternity has at least one awards ceremony a week – presumably to bolster their monstrously inflated egos. Take a fleeting look at the way the males have dressed themselves; how many badly-dressed queens do we need in Britain? Like Ozymandias, they should cry 'look on my works, ye mighty, and despair'.

But I digress. Men should shun 'fashion' because they will never crack it. More to the point, why should they bother? How often have you seen a bloke poring over the fashion pages of a magazine or a newspaper? Some chance. If he gets past page 3, it's only to check the racing results or when the football starts on the telly that evening.

Take a look at the typical club golfer, if you

can bear it. He encapsulates the average Brit's complete ignorance of fashion. He either looks like the lucky survivor of an explosion in a pizza factory, dolled up in a clashing morass of checks and stripes; or he appears to have grabbed his gardening clothes off a peg in the cellar and marched straight to the first tee. American golfers look even worse, mainly because they wear those frightful baseball caps.

Compared to the average Australian male, however, the British golfer is elegance personified: Beau Brummell compared to Sir Les Patterson, Noel Coward compared to Ned Kelly, who remains Australia's most famous person. Which sums up that peculiar country. Well, there was that cricketer, Sir Don something; he wasn't bad.

But it still beats me how the Aussie male has managed to make such a virtue out of his phenomenal scruffiness, and his loud-mouthed uncouthness. Our colonial cousins can play cricket and they can make a decent bottle of plonk, but they are, by a street of boutiques, the worst-dressed nation in the world.

Better to leave all this fashion nonsense to the Italians, who are more in tune with it. Those tight trousers and the flimsy sweaters stretched over their pasta-filled bellies suit them very nicely. Remember that in any war the Italians always have the most beautifully-cut uniforms and the least stomach for a fight.

Stick to the subfusc gear that dear old Marks and Spencer and those other High Street stores do so well; think Johnnie Major, but tone it down a bit from there. However, it seems that Mr Major is a lot more colourful than anyone imagined, isn't he? He's not all cricket and warm beer, is he? Little did we know that he'd had an affair with the former Conservative MP and Minister for Health, Edwina Currie. She made this revelation public in her *Diaries 1987 – 1992.* And why did she let the beaver out of the burrow?

You've got it – she had a book to publicize. Please read my previous remarks about brazen ladies with books and newspaper serialisations on their minds. If only we had known, when the 1997 election was being fought, that Mr Major was such a tiger in the bedroom, oh yes, I think the great British public would have cheered him home to a resounding victory over the popinjay Blair. We'll let the fragrant Lady Archer have the last words, harsh though they are, about the affair: 'I am a little surprised, not at Mrs Currie's indiscretion but at a temporary lapse in John Major's taste.'

* * *

And now Joan Bakewell has got in on the act. I was profoundly disappointed to read that in her recent autobiography she combs over the ashes of her affair with Harold Pinter – of all people. Oh, Joan, you were so lovely on the telly, how we lusted after you; you were so intelligent that we called you the 'thinking man's crumpet'.

15. HAIR AND BEAUTY

Apparently, men worry about their hair, or, to put it more accurately, they worry about the lack of it. Research has shown that men worry more about a lack of hair on their heads than they do about a lack of sex. All that consolatory rubbish that's trotted out about bald men being incredibly virile doesn't bring any consolation to Mister Baldie, and anyway he knows it's complete crap; he wants enough hair on his head to persuade the average badger to have a go at shagging it.

It's the same as all the drivel about small and large cocks. 'It's not the size, it's how you use it', runs one argument. Don't you believe it. Every man would like a bloody big cock, a whopper, a one-eyed trouser snake to make the lucky recipient's eyes water.

And whatever your crumpet says, she wants a big one to play with, too. Research has shown (please note how much selfless and unflagging work I have put into this philosophical treatise) that men think that a penis of about five inches in extent is adequate; but women think about nine inches is more their cup of tea – if I may put it delicately. In other words, women have totally different expectations about sex than do men; they also have totally different expectations about love and romance. Fellas, you'll never measure up, so don't be so bloody stupid, don't worry about it. One of my friends always maintains that *he's* never had a bad shag.

While on this subject, I must tell you about one of L'Oréal's products. That's the company which uses one of the most patronising advertising slogans ever created: 'because you're worth it', says some simpering actress. Their Elvive for Men thickening shampoo claims to 'thicken hair for better scalp coverage'. And they add: '77% of men experienced a thickening effect'. You have to wonder how they arrived at that precise figure, don't you. Anyway, it sounded a little risqué to me, because I'm a simple man, but it did prompt me to think about marketing opportunities. Soon I had started work on the 'Universal Thickening Agent for Men'. If my new process can ensure that 77% of men experience a thickening effect on their cocks, I will get very rich very quickly. I'll keep you posted on progress – but don't hold your breath.

The very fact that such a product as Elvive thickening shampoo exists shows just how

bloody stupid men are about their hair. They spend billions on hair restorer every year; in fact, our American cousins spend over one and a half billion dollars a year on hair replacement techniques. Does that surprise you? No, I'll bet it doesn't. And it's all in vain, because such an elixir does not exist. So they seek other solutions. Let's take a look at wigs – though I'd rather not because they're so very unpleasant.

Some years ago I was sitting behind an American on an airport bus. I couldn't help but notice the very obvious join between his Crown Topper (hereinafter called a CT) and his skull. It was like some nasty creeping disease; wiry strands of scrofulous ginger nylon attached to some sort of cardboard carapace – and his head moved independently of the gruesome creation. I gagged and, as soon as the aircraft took off, I had to calm myself by swallowing a great number of very large gin and tonics in quick succession.

Have you noticed that most CTs, as well as not fitting, are ginger, whatever the colour of the rest of the man's hair? I have always assumed that, long ago, a mail order company messed up its communications with a manufacturer in China or Russia or some such God-forsaken place and was landed with a huge cache of ginger wigs.

The showbiz crowd are great fans of CTs. I

learned from an impeccable source about one TV entertainer who has always used three different wigs: short, medium and long. When he's worn the long one for a couple of weeks, he announces his intention to 'pop out for a haircut' and returns wearing the shorter one. Is the man clever, stupid, or just gloriously deranged?

* * *

Men are also bloody stupid enough to spend small fortunes on more expensive solutions such as 'hair weaving'. Dear old Graham Gooch, the former England cricket captain, used to be in some of the advertisements. Did he think a light covering on his bald patch would make him more sexy? Well, think again, Graham, it makes you look like a sad old git.

That peculiar pop person, Elton John, has a mop of hair these days, after years of wearing silly hats so that we couldn't see how bald he was. Is it a CT? If it is, it's a very special model. That flowing mop atop a terminally world-weary face looks very odd to me, and rather sinister. He reminds me of a very ancient china doll, or the puppet that came to life in the William Goldman film, *Magic*.

Mind you, anyone who could sing such sickeningly sentimental lyrics as those at Princess Diana's funeral must be odd. To quote the great bard, 'how abhorred in my imagination it is! My gorge rises at it.'

* * *

You have to wonder, too, at all those really clever people who are obsessed with their hair. Robert Robinson, who chairs such amusing radio shows as 'Brain of Britain', gives the impression that he actually knows the answers to most of the questions – and maybe he does. So why does he have a Bobby Charlton comb-over?

Why did Bobby Charlton have a Bobby Charlton comb-over? He was one of England's greatest footballers and he was worried about his hair? Why? Millions of red-blooded Englishmen would have given every follicle on their bodies for a tenth of his skill – but dear old Bobby spent a lot of his time pondering how to stick his few threads of hair to his noble skull.

Sportsmen are, however, notorious for having dodgy 'barnets'. Any footballer from the 1970s looked as though a flock of magpies could take cover in their hair. Remember the seriously over-rated Kevin Keegan? Mind you, he looked as if he was in his first week of National Service compared to the Colombian footballer, Carlos Valderrama. These days most of them look like refugees from a chain gang with their shaven heads, but one or two stay true to the great tradition. There's dear David Beckham with his Alice band and his braids; what would Norman Hunter and Nobby Stiles have to say about that? Nothing printable, I feel. Beckam has several virtues as a footballer: he has a great right foot, and when he's fit he tries to give his all in every game. Unfortunately, when it comes to the really important tournaments, like the World Cup of 2002 and Euro 2004, he is shown up as a very ordinary player, as a donkey, rather than a thoroughbred.

If only Beckham devoted as much time to improving his tackling, his heading, his left foot, and his speed, as he does to his hair and his tattoos and his image, he might become a half-decent footballer. He is no longer a sportsman; he has now become a celebrity, a brand-name.

We must not forget Don King, the American boxing promoter, who, despite the time he spent in jail, has become the friend, confidant and protector of so many boxers. Boxing is a brutal sport, and it isn't his fault that, despite his warnings and ministrations, most of them have ended up penniless and broken in mind and body. However, dear old Don has one of the sporting world's most amazing hair styles. Where've you hidden the cattle prod, Don? Don't ask.

I was lucky enough to be in Madison Square Garden when Lennox Lewis first fought Evander Holyfield for the Heavyweight Championship of the World. Lewis outpointed him by a street, by the way, and was fortunate to get a draw. But I digress; the point is that the ebullient British supporters, who were there in their thousands, had the measure of the electric-haired Don. When he was introduced to the crowd, they chanted 'Oo ate all the pies?' The great promoter looked puzzled and I don't suppose any of his hangers-on, even if they were bright enough to understand, was prepared to tell him that he looked like a sack of potatoes with a coconut on top. So our great British fans reprised with 'You fat bastard, you fat bastard'. Don King got that one.

Then there's Melvyn Bragg, that excellent broadcaster and novelist. He is clearly a hair hypochondriac. I pity the poor girl who makes him up for the telly. Mel, don't be so bloody stupid.

* * *

I've got a great friend who does odd things to his hair. I love him dearly, but I wonder how he started off four years older than me and is now eight years younger. Like Melvyn, he is knocking on. But he has a huge mop of hair, which is dyed jet-black, and worn in a modified Hugh Grant style. What's the result? He looks ten years older than me – and that is very old indeed.

All these men who are neurotic about what's on top of their heads are complete pillocks, but there is no bigger pillock than the man with a pony-tail. Because it is an immutable law of nature, as fixed and unmoving as that which decrees that night follows day and *vice versa,* that the pony-tailed ones, apart from the straggly rat's-tail on the back of their heads, are always as bald as billiard balls – and they look bloody stupid.

Wigs, 'rugs', Crown Toppers, toupés, 'syrups', call them what you will, are the stock-in-trade of the showbiz brigade, and you can spot them a mile away – even on the telly. Why do they bother? Presumably they don't mind being objects of derision. But so-called cosmetic surgery is a different kettle of sick entirely.

Cosmetic surgery has been available for a long time for those rich enough and vain enough to undergo it. And few sectors of society are richer and vainer than the preening ranks of show business, among whom it has become an epidemic. It is claimed that there is hardly an actor over the age of thirty in Hollywood who has not had some 'facial re-shaping'. So much so that Hollywood film directors are complaining that the combination of surgery and Botox treatment is producing a race of frozen-faced Thespians who cannot express any emotion; some of them take several minutes of concentrated effort to raise an eyebrow. This nonsense has inevitably spread among Britain's actors, too. They should all be made to read *The Picture of Dorian Gray.*

Take a look at Burt Reynolds, who used to be a good-looking hunk, so the girls tell me.

Remember him in *The Mean Machine* and *Remembrance*? He was good, and he looked good; and he didn't look too bad in *Boogie Nights*, in which he turned in a terrific performance which earned him an Oscar nomination. In 1972, the year that *Remembrance* was made, Burt actually posed naked for the centre-fold of *Cosmopolitan Magazine* – so he must have something, mustn't he?

I am a great fan of Burt, but over the years his face has changed; his nostrils have taken on a different shape and his eyes have a somewhat oriental look. Has he fucked about with nature? I hope not because he didn't need to do so.

Not that it matters a damn, because you can only warm to a man who made the following remark about those pretentious tosspots behind the scenes in Hollywood, who kid themselves that they are 'creative artists'. Good old Burt said: 'Having done three hundred television shows and almost sixty movies, I'm tired of guys who are younger than some sandwiches I've had telling me to turn left at the couch. There's no appreciation of actors and no sense of history.'

* * *

Dear old Cliff Richard, the Queen Mum of pop, has definitely been messing about with his face;

as he admitted to *OK! Magazine,* he's had himself Botoxed. His forehead is as smooth as a baby's bum and never moves an inch. Cliff, you've been bloody stupid.

Never mind, I love these 'luvvies' and want to write a film for them. Burt and Cliff could be two buddies, dashing and macho. Cher, who has re-shaped her looks under the surgeon's knife and needle, and is honest enough to refer to herself as 'the plastic surgery poster girl', could play the female lead – and the two lads could fancy her like mad. OK, OK, this is show business and it requires a monumental suspension of disbelief. Bear with me, please.

A newcomer to the movies would also be in the cast; she's Jocelyne Wildenstein, who married into that phenomenally rich family, lost the affections of her husband, Alec, and decided to re-create herself as the 'Cat Woman' so that he would love her again; apparently dear old Alec loved big cats. After countless operations and millions of dollars spent on re-modelling her, well, her everything, she became known as the Bride of Wildenstein. And it all ended in the extreme sadness of divorce – just because Jocelyne claimed that she caught her husband in bed with a young model. It just goes to show that not every man in this mad world is bloody stupid. Mind you, he had to agree to pay her about £100,000 a month as part of the divorce settlement.

Anyway, Jocelyne, the Bride of Wildenstein, will have an important part, maybe as Cliff Richard's Mum. And so will Michael Jackson. Wacko Jacko has changed himself out of recognition since his days as one of the Jackson Five. It's such a pity that his nose is falling off his face; still, you can't have everything in life.

All we need now is a title. It's got to be a musical and maybe Elton John could be signed up to write it, because he would fit in so well. How about *A Little Knife Music*, *Funny Face 2*, *Theatre of Blood 2*, *Oh What a Lovely Scar*, *Rocky Horror Picture Show 2*, *Born to Botox*, *From Hair to Eternity*. Oh, and *Vanity Fair* of course. Your suggestions, dear reader, would be welcomed.

However, I've let myself digress. Forget the musical and mark, learn and inwardly digest.

IMPORTANT LESSON NUMBER SIXTEEN

Make the best of what nature has given you. Hair extensions and face freezing are as useless as penis extensions– something that Burt certainly didn't need, did he? If you don't believe me, ask John Wayne Bobbit.

It is often said that time is a great healer. OK, but it is also cruel and unforgiving and nobody can beat it. The last word on this subject comes from one of our great poets, Mr Wystan Hugh Auden; if anyone ever wanted a face-lift, by the way, it was him. His mug looked like a relief map of Birmingham, but he wasn't bothered because he had his writing and his shirt-lifting to occupy his mind and body. He wrote:

'O let not Time deceive you,
You cannot conquer Time.

In the burrows of the Nightmare
Where Justice naked is,
Time watches from the shadow
And coughs when you would kiss.'

In other words, heed IMPORTANT LESSON NUMBER SIXTEEN, and don't be so bloody stupid.

16. OTHER FOIBLES WHICH MEN SHOULD AVOID

Baseball caps. They are for men who drive white vans, who look at the pictures in *The Sun*, and whose lips move when they try to read the captions.

Back-to-front baseball caps. These are for children and Australians.

Cut-off trousers and T-shirts with slogans. These are for children and Australians.

Denim bomber jackets. If you still possess one of these, give it a safe haven in the dressing-up box, or burn it.

Jewellery. Hairdressers, bouncers and dodgy geezers who sell second-hand cars wear bracelets, 'gold' medallions around their necks, and sovereign rings. The only jewellery a man should wear is a handsome watch and unobtrusive cufflinks.

Tattoos. See above, particularly under 'jewellery' and 'baseball caps'.

Corsets. If you think a corset will disguise a fat gut, think again, because it can be spotted a mile away and deserves only the severest form of mockery.

Personalised number plates. I saw a man get into a Mercedes the other day and his number plate read PMT 1. Hasn't he seen people snickering at him and his car? Don't even think about buying such an abomination as a personalised number plate. It's easy for witnesses to remember, for a start.

And it might do you out of a shag. I know a woman 'of a certain age', who is very keen on a regular bout of horizontal jogging. Recently her eye alighted on a young-ish bloke called Nigel and he was right in the frame for a spot of mattress dancing – that is, until she saw the number plate on his car, which read NIGELP. His status immediately changed from sex object to total wanker.

17. SHOPPING

Men and women are completely incompatible as shoppers. On the one hand, men have a defined objective when they go shopping; they are practical and speedy. They want that kind of wine, those golf clubs, that pair of trousers or that sweater in that colour. You can call it tunnel vision, if you wish, but I call it knowing what you want and going out to get it.

To a woman, however, shopping is an end in itself; it's a hobby, it's relaxation, it's almost a profession, in an amateur sort of way. It's certainly therapy and the media encourages them to think of it in that way. I've lost count of the number of times I've seen the expression, 'retail therapy', in the newspapers – it usually precedes some simple-minded article about a new range of handbags for £1500 apiece, or knickers 'designed' by some showbiz trollop at £500 a leg.

Women can go shopping for a whole day – and enjoy it, that is the astonishing thing. I have a friend whose ex-wife used to fly to Hong Kong 'for the shopping' – small wonder that she's now an ex-wife.

In contrast, the average man believes that ten minutes is just enough time to shop for a new suit and a pair of shoes, and that the weekly supermarket ordeal can be done and dusted in fifteen minutes flat.

You will, on occasion, have to go shopping with your wife/partner. There is no point in trying to avoid it, so make the best of it. But make sure that you divide the shopping into two lists. Your list has all the interesting items: the cheese, the bread, the shellfish, and of course, the wine. She does all the staples: fruit and veg, dishwasher salt, Persil, cat food, lavatory cleaner and paper, baked beans, and so on; I'm sure you've got the general idea.

Never, ever attempt the weekly shop on your own; there is no more heart-rending sight than a man at large on his own in a supermarket on a Saturday morning. He is John Wayne without his Colt 45, Tiger Woods without his golf glove, John Prescott without the keys to one of his Jags, Tony Blair without 'a new initiative'. He makes a distressing spectacle, bereft of initiative and spirit – and especially when he pauses in one of the aisles, gets his fumbling mitts on his mobile and starts to ask agitated questions about which brand of baby gloop to buy. Don't be so bloody stupid, you shouldn't be there on your own, in fact you shouldn't be there at all, this is WOMAN'S WORK. See preceding chapters 5,6,7,8 and 9.

IMPORTANT LESSON NUMBER SEVENTEEN

Make a virtue of necessity and play to your strengths.

There can be some consolations, however. If you look helpless enough, some women, if they are not too lathered in their own misery at having to shop for so-called essentials when all they want to do is waste a few grand on uncomfortable shoes and unsuitable clothing, will take pity on you. Research shows that the freezer section is the best place in a supermarket for picking up, or being picked up by, women. Anywhere in Peter Jones, in Sloane Square in London, is just as good a place for picking up, or being picked up by, women.

IMPORTANT LESSON NUMBER EIGHTEEN

A bit of spare is never too far away – even in a supermarket.

18. WORK

Unfortunately, this is something that has to be done; not many of us have been born with the proverbial and much-envied silver spoon firmly clenched between the toothless gums. Unlike royalty, we don't have someone to press the toothpaste on to our toothbrushes, nor someone to iron the fiver for the church collection plate. Though I do know one lucky man who does his usual morning ablutions and leaves his wife to clean up the mess – the foamy dribbles of his toothpaste, the fine patina of slime from his shave and his wash, his nose-hair clippings, the thick layer of scum around his bath, and presumably his nail clippings as well. But I believe he does flush the lavatory on his own, and I know for a fact that she never goes near his donger. Anyway, he is a man to admire, because he has got away with it for years and is still getting away with it. Well done, old chap.

* * *

However, let's get back to the subject of work and how you can avoid it. You can always try and pick a very successful woman from the crowd, woo her, marry her and then live off her money; a high-flying lawyer, for example, or a woman who has built up her own business, or who is in charge of a business that someone else has built up. There are inherent problems with this strategy in that you must accept the proviso that, if you are to stay firmly seated on the gravy train, you must love, honour and, above all, obey her. This can be tricky, since she is supposed to do all those things for you.

Then there is the awful danger that eventually she'll get broody, announce that she wants four children in quick time, and will then devote herself to their well-being and upbringing. You are really in the mire then, just when you were getting really comfortable.

You could marry late, having selected a successful career woman who has adult children. This isn't a bad plan in theory, but in practice it is fraught with future dangers; for a start you will have to try to be nice to her ghastly children and they will hate you anyway, however hard you try to be Mister Nice Guy. A better plan is to set your sights on a successful career woman who is not only childless but who is more or less past child-bearing age.

If this rich woman fails to materialize, here

are some IMPORTANT LESSONS which may help to alleviate the pain of working for a living.

IMPORTANT LESSON NUMBER NINETEEN

Don't take work seriously.

IMPORTANT LESSON NUMBER TWENTY

Work smart, don't work hard.

IMPORTANT LESSON NUMBER TWENTY-ONE

Never, ever, work for a woman.

Most of them are nuts anyway, and especially so when they are in a position of power. They actually believe the old chestnut that women at work must do things twice as well as men in order to be thought half as effective. Good, let's keep it that way.

The trouble is that, if you accept the incontrovertible wisdom of IMPORTANT LESSON NUMBER TWENTY-ONE, there are several businesses in which you will be unable to work. Take the media in its broadest sense, for a start. All those businesses – publishing, radio, television – are dominated by women, and the great majority of those women are of the feminazi persuasion. Even the *Sun*, that fearless propagator of macho male concerns, the creator of the Page Three girl, the newspaper that sees the world through a beery haze of tits, bums and 'lunch-boxes', now has a female editor.

Can you believe that men can be so bloody stupid? Yes, I'm talking to you, Rupert Murdoch. It won't be long before the tits go out of the window, and in will come Lifestyle, Gardening, and *SunFem* supplements. What will all the white-van-men and builders in Britain do then? They won't switch to the *Indie* and the *Grauniad,* Rupe, that's for sure; they'll buy another 'Red Top' like the *Mirror.*

* * *

The delicate world of book publishing is larded with Sophies, Harriets, Emmas and Annabels. Don't even bother to try and sell them a novel with an ordinary bloke in it, someone who likes to go out boozing and shagging; it will go straight to the bottom of the slush pile. Just make sure that your hero is as sensitive as the average Mayfair art dealer or dress designer and they might just read a few pages – and then they'll send it back anyway.

And then there's television. Have you ever wondered why every man in every 'soap' and every situation comedy is shown as a congenital idiot, as a work-shy incompetent, as a sexual no-hoper, as a pathetic wanker with a brain the size of a neutered tom-cat's bollocks? It's because women control almost every aspect of the commissioning, development and production of such programmes. Come on, guys, don't be so pathetic, empower yourselves, don't be so bloody stupid.

By the way, if a malign fate casts a giant and evil shadow over you in the form of a female boss, do not delude yourself with the thought that your cunning plan – to charver your way into a cast-iron position of influence – will stand the remotest prospect of long-term success. There is a sporting chance that you will throw your leg over her, and she will then set about sucking you dry, so to speak. And the inevitable scheme of things is as follows: one fine day, you will stride into her office, your dick in your hand as usual, but, instead of rogering her rotten (and in the firm's time, too), you will walk out of there, shell-shocked and limp-dicked, your P45 in your hand, and on a desolate one-way trip to the Job Centre.

It's now time to return to IMPORTANT LESSONS NUMBERS NINETEEN and TWENTY. Don't take work seriously and work smart, not hard.

I can show you how to become seriously rich. It's simple – get yourself lots of directorships. This can't be difficult; take a look at the calibre of the directors of public companies and you will understand why I make that statement. It is an immutable law of business that the more directorships you procure, the more you will be offered. Take every one. Before you know it, people will start talking about you in hushed and serious tones as having 'a safe pair of hands'. And you will need a safe pair – to grab all that lovely money and take it home safely.

The time then comes when you must be very careful. You are getting seriously rich, but you know it's all bullshit; you are not a genius, you are not Superman, you've been lucky, perhaps a bit ruthless. In your heart of hearts, you realise that you don't deserve the obscenely inflated fees paid to you by the various companies whose boardrooms you visit a couple of times a year.

However, this is not the time for guilt feelings, you plonker. Now is not the time to let down all the other passengers on the gravy train. Now is the time to play the game – if I may be allowed to mix my metaphors yet again. The party line is simple and incontrovertible: you must give the impression that you live, sleep, eat, drink and breathe only for the good of the companies you serve – and that you deserve every penny you get.

Since you have now become one of our 'Captains of Industry', you might even, with a bit of luck, become the subject of one of those fawning newspaper profiles. This is roughly how it will go:

'Mr C gets out of bed at 5am, reads all the broadsheet newspapers by 6am, and then does a five-mile run – in under thirty minutes. Next, he watches CNN News and the Bloomberg Channel while tackling his organic wheaties and orange juice, and is driven to his office. While he's sitting in his car, he makes phone calls. He's in his office by 7am, has his first meeting at 7.05am, has attended another dozen important meetings by noon, many of which are about company strategy, has bought and sold ten major businesses over lunch (just a salad and some sparkling water) and then repeats the whole process through the afternoon.'

You must ignore the sour and envious buggers who say things like: 'who does this arsehole think he's kidding?' or 'who does the sad git phone at 7am and I hope whoever it is tells him to get stuffed.' This kind of publicity is invaluable and should bring in several more offers of directorships. Take them.

Toe the party line like all the others, the businessmen who proudly proclaim that they are 'workaholics'. Don't start questioning why anyone in his right mind would wish to own up to such a vice, let alone take pride in it. Ignore those jealous souls who scathingly refer to the 'workaholic' as a pathetic creation of the last century or so, someone who takes refuge from the reality of life, who hides from its real challenges, its pleasures, and its fun by immersing himself in work; who maintain that he is only half a human being, a frightened twat who lacks perspective and, therefore, cannot be trusted to make good decisions about anything.

Some time ago, I read one of those obsequious articles about a certain Chief Executive. On reading the article, I recalled that I owned shares in the company and I suppose I should have been pleased that the firm was in the hands of a man apparently so brilliant and so devoted to its cause, yet another self-confessed 'workaholic'. However, I allowed my contrarian leanings to hold sway and on the following morning I sold the shares, since I had no confidence in a Chief Executive who was clearly such a pompous pillock.

Let's take a look at some of the Supermen of British business (all of them being fine and upstanding men of good reputation) and see what we can learn from their supreme ability to make money – for themselves. Note that the following examples come from the years 2002 to 2003; I am indebted to *The*

Independent newspaper for much of the ensuing information, in an article of 24 April, 2003.

1. During the last financial year, Reuters paid over £2million in management bonuses to the clever chaps who managed to lose £498million of the company's money; these directors and managers also presided over a share price fall of 70%. They still got their money, and the shareholders did not stop them.

2. Adam Singer of the cable firm, Telewest, got a pay-off of £1.8million a year or so ago. For what? While he was in charge, the share price dropped from £5.60 to just over 2p, and 1500 staff lost their jobs.

3. During the year 2002 to 2003, the oil company, Shell, saw its share price slump by 27% under the guidance of Sir Philip Watts, and he laid down his plans to sack 4000 people. And his pay increased by over 50% to £1.8million a year; oh, and over a million quid went into his pension as well. Early in 2004 he was forced to admit that he had made a complete bollocks of estimating the company's oil reserves. However, he had the good grace to leave the company.

4. Matt Barrett, CEO of Barclays Bank, has done

one of the best deals. If he loses his job for any reason, he will receive a 'golden good-bye' of £5million. I am not very sophisticated in comparison with these very clever businessmen, but rewarding someone for failure doesn't seem quite right.

5. This deal pales into insignificance compared to the one proposed for a certain Monsieur Jean-Pierre Garnier, the chief executive of GlaxoSmithKline. Apart from an estimated salary of over £4million last year – how many packets of Gauloise and bottles of plonk do you need, J-P? – it was proposed that his going away present would total between £15million and £22million. These frogs have got a cheek, haven't they? Amazingly, the ungrateful shareholders voted against his pay package; shame on you.

6. Then, there is Michael Dobson, the Chief Executive of Schroders, the fund manager. Their shares lost a quarter of their value in the last year and 500 staff got their P45s. What about Mike, though? Yes, he got a salary and bonuses of £3million.

7. Finally, we come to Allan Leighton, who has the very important job of Chairman of the Royal Mail Group, whose well-being and effectiveness is important to us all. Mr Leighton presides over a business which, towards the end of 2003, had lost £1.8billion in the previous two years – and those figures were made public by Adam Crozier, the Chief Executive. That adds up to a lot of losses, doesn't it? In fact, if my mental arithmetic is correct, it amounts to the little matter of £2.4million a day. You might think that Allan Leighton would concentrate on alleviating those losses and making Royal Mail into a profitable concern again. Well, you would be wrong, because he has nine other jobs. We must assume, therefore, that Allan Leighton is a genius, another Superman, mustn't we?

A slight digression on the subject of the mail is allowable, I think. In May, 2004, Mr Leighton announced that the Royal Mail had managed to make an operating profit of over £200 million. Are congratulations in order? Hardly. Any fool can make a profit if, when your business is in deep trouble, you are allowed the simple expedients of raising your prices, of sacking several thousand of your workers, and reducing the service you offer. The Royal Mail spin doctors have told us that the second postal delivery has been abandoned; in fact, it's the first postal delivery which has been abandoned.

In other words, the poor old British public is paying a lot more for a lot less. It's easy when you know how, eh? The Royal Mail, by the way, failed to hit any of their fifteen performance targets. I note that the area in which I live is the second worst place in Britain for postal deliveries; if we're lucky, the post arrives by lunchtime. I also note that Labour MPs castigated Royal Mail for providing a 'Third World' service. It's not even that good.

Nevertheless, there were bonuses all round for the Royal Mail executives, although Mr Leighton had the good sense to postpone his. Not so the Chief Executive, Adam Crozier. On top of his salary of £500,000, he tucked away a bonus of £300,000.

Decades ago, my wife and I were very lucky to have our letters delivered by a postman called Ted. He showed great pride in his job, as did so many of his colleagues in those days. For example, I remember that, on our return from a holiday, we found all our letters neatly arranged in bundles, and in date order.

Do you think that Messrs. Leighton and Crozier would have been fit to lace the admirable Ted's standard-issue Post Office boots? Answers on a postcard, please.

* * *

However, to get back to the main theme of this chapter, I would not dream of saying what some people, livid with the green-eyed monster, say, that most of the businessmen who purport to run large public companies have got their snouts so far into the trough that you can't even see their heels.

It is of course a nice cosy game played by Big Business and you want to make sure you are a part of it. It goes like this. The Chief Executive of Joe Bloggs plc appoints a few mates as non-executive directors and they vote through his huge salary and benefits package. In turn, those non-executive directors put the Joe Bloggs Chief Executive on to their Boards of Directors and he helps to vote through their huge salary and benefits packages. You scratch my back and I'll scratch yours, out with the vintage champagne, and fuck the shareholders.

It reminds me of the song in *Oh, What a Lovely War*:

> 'One staff officer jumped over another staff officer's back,
> And another staff officer jumped over another staff officer's back,'
> Etc. etc.
> 'They were only playing leapfrog,
> They were only playing leapfrog ...'

* * *

In contrast, there is Sir Ken Morrison, who has run William Morrison Supermarkets for nearly fifty years. He can't be that bright because he concentrates on that job alone. However, since the company went public in 1967, he has been responsible for 36 years of unbroken sales and profit growth; though the problems caused by his recent acquisition of Safeway may spoil his remarkable record of success. However, the point is that he does not grab directorships like a starving gorilla who sees a bunch of bananas for the first time in several days; and he pays himself a relatively modest annual salary. Come on, Ken, you're letting all the other blokes on the gravy train down, get your snout in the trough, old son. Greed is good, as Gordon Gekko taught us in the film, *Wall Street*.

Here is a footnote to my remarks about business. Once upon a time, I worked for an American who made himself pre-eminent in his own specialized field. He was clever and dedicated and was about as human as a robot. However, he wasn't content with success alone but set out to manufacture a legend of his own brilliance and industriousness– and a lot of people believed it. For example, he told people that he divided his working day into fifteen-minute segments and worked from 5 o'clock in the morning until 11 at night. I was one of the few people who didn't believe the myth because I attended several meetings through which he slept.

IMPORTANT LESSON NUMBER TWENTY-TWO

Always have your bullshit meter turned on and highly tuned.

19. POLITICIANS AND LAWYERS

Tony Blair qualified as a lawyer before he became a professional politician; and for many people he probably embodies all that they loathe and distrust about both professions.

For a start, there's something about the idea of a 'professional politician' that makes my flesh creep. Politics shouldn't be a profession; it should be something you do out of conviction, i.e. not to exercise power, nor to get filthy rich. Just for a moment contrast the likes of Blair, Gordon Brown and John Prescott with Roy Jenkins, Harold Macmillan and Winston Churchill. Three 'professional politicians' against three men whose remarkably varied talents enriched the life of this and other nations, and who could have succeeded in any of a number of different professions. No contest.

In allowing myself a short digression about Tony Blair, the lawyer and professional politician,

How can you take anyone seriously, let alone Britain's Prime Minister, who allows 'a lifestyle adviser' through his front door? OK, Carole Caplin, the preposterous former topless model, had her marching orders from the portals of number 10, but what was she doing there in the first place? And she even got her dodgy Aussie boyfriend, Peter Foster, in on the action; he was swaggering around doing property deals for Mrs Blair.

One assumes that the fragrant Carole was on the Blairs' payroll at the behest of Cherie, who, even though she is a lawyer, appears to have some basic intelligence. But, under Caplin's influence, she was carrying on like a menopausal bimbo, seemingly willing to imbibe any amount of mumbo jumbo in order to rescue her fading looks. Except that she hasn't. In fact, when she is seen in public, she appears to have dressed in the dark – and in someone else's clothes.

It is hardly a surprise to hear that La Caplin is ready to spill the beans about what really goes on in the Prime Minister's household. What did Tony and Cherie expect? Common sense and loyalty?

While we are talking about the Blairs' friends, let's consider Alastair Campbell, Tony's erstwhile right-hand man, his 'professor of spin', the person who really ran this country for several years. He also received his P45 from Tony, and

(AN INFANT LAWYER!)

he's another close associate who is ready to spill his guts about life at Number 10. Big Al has been widely quoted as seeing his diaries as his pension, and they should guarantee him a very prosperous old age. Yet again, how could our Prime Minister put his trust in a former tabloid journalist like Campbell; he reminds me of nothing so much as the manager of a Conference League football club – but without the dress sense.

With friends like these, Tony Blair surely doesn't need any enemies. That old saying brings me to …

IMPORTANT LESSON NUMBER TWENY-THREE

If you surround yourself with arseholes, they will eventually shit on you.

One final thought about poor old Tony; despite the fact that he has as much *gravitas* as freshly-spun candy-floss, I suspect that he fancies himself as a great leader, a modern Churchill, a latter-day Shakespearean hero, particularly after his quasi-triumphant progress, clinging on to Bush's coat-tails, in Iraq, although the gloss has long since gone from that exercise in *realpolitik*. With his oratorical style, let's imagine how he would have got on with a couple of the great calls to arms.

1. Winston Churchill. Well, look, uh, I'll be honest with you, we've got to look after our island, whatever the cost; mind you, I suppose Gordon will haul me over the coals for that remark. Obviously, we'll have a bit of a go at them on the beaches, yer know, and I must remind you that some of our beaches have Blue Flag awards for cleanliness. And in the fields. I mean, we don't give a bugger what the farmers and those other people out in the countryside think anyway. And in the streets, uh well, I say to you that, yer know, they'll be a bit of a no-go area, that I can promise.

2. William Shakespeare's Henry V. Well, look, uh, sort of, into the breach again, eh? And I'm not referring to Cherie, ha, ha. Or close it up with, uh, dead people. I'm sorry but there's no easy way to say it. Obviously, war, yer know, brings casualties, so long as it's not one of my own lot. I mean there's no point in buying a flat from an Aussie con-man for the number one son, if he's going to be turned into dog meat in Iraq, is there? So, come on, obviously, we've simply got to stiffen everything up, summon up the blood, yer know. On second thoughts, over to you, John Major, that seems to be your department. Ha, ha.

Research has shown that not many people like lawyers (nor estate agents, nor politicians); that's worth repeating at regular intervals, like a mantra, whatever that is. And I repeat that Tony Blair trained as a lawyer. The long-standing popularity of the following joke helps to emphasise the enduring low repute of such people.

Question: how would you describe a thousand lawyers at the bottom of the sea?
Answer: a bloody good start.

Here again we must quote Shakespeare. In Henry VI, Part 2, Cade spouts about his idyllic world where 'when I am king … there shall be no money; all shall eat and drink on my score; and I will apparel them all in one livery, that they may agree like brothers, and worship me their lord.' It's a dream that most people have dreamed but the more practical Dick replies: 'the first thing we do, let's kill all the lawyers.'

Most of us would cheer his words to the echo. It leads us neatly into the next chapter, which is about divorce.

20. DIVORCE

I have already told you about an unmarried friend of mine who, whenever the subject of marriage or divorce crops up, with invariable smugness shouts out the old maxim of bachelors the world over, 'the cheapest fuck is the one you pay for'. There is more than a grain of truth in the remark, but many couples start out idealistic enough to think that they can live together in peace and harmony, and that the whole will become stronger than the two parts. Some even achieve their aims; as I have said before, I know three or four happily married couples.

However, last year in the UK roughly 150,000 couples were divorced. Just imagine how many more than that number are living in misery and planning a divorce – or murder. The latter course of action, even if extreme when compared to the trauma of a divorce, might be worth the risk. Certainly, I have heard men in the midst of a divorce state emphatically that they would like to murder the lawyers involved in the case; and not just their wives' lawyers but also their own.

A divorce is one of the most lucrative cash cows that the average blood-sucking weasel of a lawyer can milk. It is in his or her interest to stretch out the proceedings as long as humanly possible while the till gets red-hot with the cash being stuffed inside it by the poor bastards who are trying to get out of their lousy marriages.

By the way, I must state here that my favourite lawyer, Nigel B, is exempted from all past, current and future criticisms of his profession. And my missus says I must also exclude another lawyer, Dorothy H, from such nasty remarks.

However, this is no time to be sloppy and sentimental, so here's another lawyer joke. Please feel free to substitute estate agents or politicians for lawyers, if you wish.

Question: what do you think of a thousand lawyers buried up to their necks in sand?
Answer: not enough sand.

Or as George Bernard Shaw put it more elegantly: 'All professions are conspiracies against the laity.'

* * *

However, let's get back to the main drift of the

discourse. If you are a man, it's advisable to avoid divorce at all costs. When it becomes inevitable, resign yourself to being taken to the cleaners by the woman who was once your nearest and dearest. Resign yourself to sweating blood to keep her in the style to which she grew accustomed while she was your wife – because the legal system is totally and utterly rigged in her favour, especially in Britain, where the divorce laws are almost as biased in favour of women as those in the USA.

Apparently, there were just over a quarter of a million marriages in the UK in the year 2000, compared with about 425,000 in 1972. To my mind, it's a wonder that there were any at all, because when the marriage hits choppy seas and then founders, it's the man who will try to survive in the dark and fathomless waters – above all, it's he who will do the paying.

In my selfless efforts to help all those men in the throes of divorce, I have been researching the subject wherever I can, and I found some material on the Internet – which probably means it's grossly inaccurate. Nevertheless, some of the basic tenets are as follows: there are *no* firm rules about how a couple's assets are to be divided; there is no presumption that the value of the marital home and any other property will be split equally between the parties; and the law should not treat husbands differently to wives.

Don't you believe a word of it. The golden rule and rock-like presumption is that the wife is the injured party; and the other firm and most important rule is that the wife will get at least half of the property, including any owned before the marriage – that is, if there's anything left after the solicitors have taken their cuts. And the wife's lawyers will go for everything, including your wine and your car, and a share of your future earnings and your pension. In other words, you can look forward to working your bollocks off to keep your ex in Versace clothes and Jimmy Choo shoes until, exhausted, you topple into your grave.

You might try to salt some money away, but this can misfire; I read recently about a man who hid £150,000 from his first wife pending their divorce. The dimwit was found out because he told his second wife about it and, guess what, she spilled the beans when they got divorced. He was sentenced to eighteen months in jail for that bit of deception; a bit over the top, I feel, but why was he so bloody stupid?

I heard about another loser who was about to undergo a divorce and he left about twenty grand in a locker at his golf club, a rather snooty one near London. Unfortunately, the clubhouse burned down and he lost the money. Not much chance of an insurance claim there, eh?

* * *

However, back to the ex-wife. If she chooses not to work, you will have to pay to maintain her for as long as she lives – and she will undoubtedly petition the courts for more money in the future and, believe me, she will get it.

She can also live with another man in what used to be your house, at your expense and you will not be able to get any recompense, even though you know that the bloke who's shagging your ex (not that you care about that) is sharing their living costs. In comparison, you won't have much chance of doing any charvering because you won't be able to afford to go out. Your entertainment will amount to no more than a couple of cans of supermarket own-label beer and a take-away in front of the TV.

So, try and go for a clean break when you get divorced, although this is getting more and more difficult to achieve. It will hurt mightily at the time, and you may have to sell everything you own, but it will be worth it in the long run. My final thought on the subject is that it's about time we returned to the state of affairs as summarised by the celebrated 18th-century jurist, William Blackstone: 'the interests of husband and wife are one – and that one is the husband.' Good on you, Bill.

Important Lesson Number Twenty-four

Never admit a thing. If your wife catches you *in flagrante* with her best friend, remain calm, get your kit back on, and deny everything. Later, you can claim mistaken identity.

Important Lesson Number Twenty-five

If you catch your wife doing a bit on the side, pretend you haven't. Hold the evidence in reserve until you can use it to your own advantage. Remember: knowledge is power.

21. COUNSELLING

A whole new industry called Counselling has been created over the last few years. In the mid-seventies the British Association of Counselling had a few hundred members, but now has over 16,000. An even more blood-curdling statistic is that it is estimated that well over 100,000 people work as full-time and part-time 'counsellors' in Britain; and that more than a million 'counselling encounters', whatever they are, take place each month.

It is my firm view that not one of these so-called counsellors is fit to serve a cup of skinny *latte* to Frasier Crane, let alone counsel anyone about anything.

If someone steals your garden gnomes one Saturday night, the police will send you a letter offering counselling. If you fall over and sprain your ankle, you will be offered it, and twenty lawyers will want to handle your case against whomever they can claim caused you to fall. The fact that you were pissed at the time and that it was your own stupid fault doesn't count for anything, because, in this day and age, you cannot be at fault; someone else must always take the blame. However foolish your actions, you are not required to take any responsibility for them. As soon as there is an accident, for example, those cretins who are mistakenly called counsellors come out of the woodwork and make matters incomparably worse.

It makes one wonder what has happened to those great virtues of self-reliance and fortitude. Once upon a time we were taught, both by precept and example, that they were the essential traits in the British character that marked us out from the rest of the world, that made us different and a bit special. Now we are being moulded into a nation of navel-gazing emotional cripples. Of course that will make us all so much easier to control; people who use their brains and have moral courage are not easy to manipulate and are therefore anathema to the contemporary politician and bureaucrat.

The outburst of public hysteria after the death of Diana, Princess of Wales, was yet another aspect of this pathetic lack of self-control and sense of proportion. The sight of all those people 'grieving', like paid professional wailers from less fortunate parts of the globe, made me sick to the stomach. The emotions on display were false, and deplorable; and just as deplorable were the cynical efforts of the Gutter Press to inflame those emotions, and to denigrate the Royal Family for not joining in the general hysteria. As for all those bloody bunches of flowers, with their inane messages, which cluttered up Kensington Gardens ...

The much-quoted movie magnate, Sam Goldwyn, was right on target when he said: 'Anyone who goes to a psychiatrist ought to have his head examined.' Another Hollywood legend, the great crime writer Raymond Chandler, described psychiatry as 'fifty per cent bunk, thirty per cent fraud, ten per cent parrot talk, and the remaining ten per cent just a fancy lingo for the common sense we have had for hundreds of years.'

I would say that anyone who has anything to do with a counsellor ought to be taken away and left under an ice-cold shower until he comes to his senses. Don't be so bloody stupid.

There has been a great deal of research about the effects of psychotherapy (studies by Hans Eysenk fifty years ago, by Lester Luborsky, and by Strupp and Hadley in the 1970s, and by Dr William Piper in 1991). Their basic conclusions have been that counselling, even by real professionals, does more harm than good. Just talk to a sympathetic friend; that friend will only cost you a bottle or two of wine, and will help you. A so-called counsellor will fuck you up.

I once wrote an article entitled 'An ounce of friendship is worth a ton of counselling'. It was in response to some half-baked witterings from Relate, which used to be called the Marriage Guidance Council; and please note how a straightforward self-explanatory name was changed to one which kow-tows to contemporary psycho-babble and to gutless political correctness. Suffice to say that I hold fast to my opinion as expressed above. If your marriage is in trouble, don't go near a counsellor, because if you do a potential disaster that is just a distant thrum over the far horizon will inevitably become a destructive juggernaut rushing unstoppably towards you.

22. RELATIONSHIPS

As soon as someone wants to discuss his or her 'relationship' with you, you might as well accept the fact that the relationship is probably over – so, it's not worth talking about.

I am lucky in having a number of close friends and my relationships with them have stood the test of time. Over the several decades I have known them, we have argued the toss about all manner of things, both frivolous and serious; we have had some fierce disagreements and have even come close to physical violence at times; and we have mostly had enormous fun together.

I cannot recall ever discussing my relationship with a single one of them – and some of them are women, for God's sake.

A few months ago, I was sitting in a restaurant in San Francisco and, because the tables were very close together, couldn't help overhearing some of the next door conversation between a couple of 30-something Americans;

I think one was male and the other was female, but it was hard to tell. It was all about their relationship, and how their relationships with friends they had in common affected their relationship. When they started peering into their navels and scratching the zits they thought they found there, I was hoping to hear some juicy tales of adultery, or maybe buggery, sodomy and other interestingly deviant practices. But these two no-hopers were the most excruciatingly boring people on whom I have eavesdropped in years – because they were discussing relationships.

THE "RELATIONSHIP HIGHWAY-CODE" FOR MEN

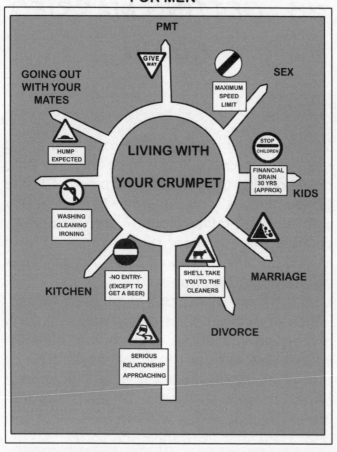

23. GETTING MARRIED AGAIN

Second marriages rarely work and third marriages never do. And is there anything more heart-breaking than charting the progress of one of your friends who has gone for the 'trophy wife' the second time around? She's thirty years younger than the poor sap she's married, and blonde because that's *de rigueur*. Actually, she's an 'aeroplane blonde' – there's a black box below. Then there's the permanent suntan, which must be topped up by frequent, long and expensive holidays, and, darling, she must have a 4x4 vehicle. Nothing beats a bit of posing at the traffic lights in a 4x4, mobile phone pressed to the ear under the bottle-blonde tresses. Yes, I know it's illegal, but you don't think that stops them, do you?

And naturally a personal trainer is absolutely essential.

She 'just loves all Bill's friends'; well, she does

until the wedding is over. It's not long before she hates all Bill's friends and she's screwing the personal trainer, while poor old Bill slaves away to earn the money to keep up with her expensive tastes in clothes, cars and holidays.

For a while, poor old Bill is just besotted enough with his new trophy to try to keep up with her, so he runs himself haggard trying to get fit, and keep the weight down. Eventually, he may even have to submit to the indignity of matching tracksuits.

Then she wants his babies. Soon, she wants a divorce. And the merry-go-round starts again.

FINAL IMPORTANT LESSON

You can't afford it. So, don't be so bloody stupid.